S0-ABC-388

1C/G

1C/G

ONE-COLOR GRAPHICS

THE POWER OF CONTRAST

SELECTED BY CHEN DESIGN ASSOCIATES

GLOUCESTER MASSACHUSETTS

ROCKPORT PUBLISHERS

First published in the United States of America by
Rockport Publishers, Inc.
33 Commercial Street
Gloucester, Massachusetts 01930-5089
Telephone: (978) 282-9590
Fax: (978) 283-2742
www.rockpub.com

ISBN 1-56496-923-1

10 9 8 7 6 5 4 3 2 1

Design: Chen Design Associates, San Francisco, CA

Printed in China

DEDICATION

To Pam, Rachel, and Ethan, who have patiently spent many late nights without me.

Thanks to all the gifted people past and present who have contributed their passions to CDA. We're privileged and honored to cross creative paths with you.

Thank you to Kristin, David, and Cora at Rockport Publishers for the support; to Jo, Matt, and Michael for helping us on judging day; and all the designers whose projects are included in this collection — thank you for your inspiration.

JC

CONTENTS

NEXT PAGE

★★★★★★★

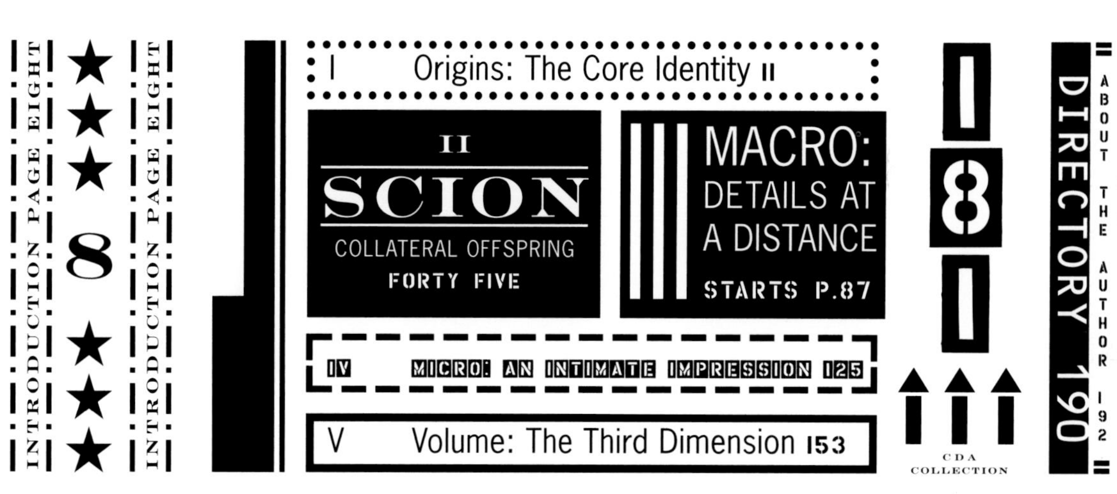
INTRODUCTION PAGE EIGHT
8
INTRODUCTION PAGE EIGHT
I Origins: The Core Identity 11
II
SCION
COLLATERAL OFFSPRING
FORTY FIVE
III
MACRO:
DETAILS AT
A DISTANCE
STARTS P.87
IV MICRO: AN INTIMATE IMPRESSION 125
V Volume: The Third Dimension 153
8
CDA
COLLECTION
DIRECTORY 190
ABOUT THE AUTHOR 192

THE POWER OF ONE

The first man on the moon

A young John Jr. saluting his father's coffin

The invention of the wheel

Rosa Parks's refusal to move from her seat

A Shakespearean monologue

A solitary student facing a tank in Tiananmen Square

One person believing the earth is round

LIMITS. EVERYONE HATES THE WORD.
Do you drive the speed limit? Are we encouraged as children to settle for less? "More is better," "The sky's the limit," and "You can have it all!"—these are just a few of the cultural values we blindly inherit from the dreamers who preceded us. As creatives, why settle for just one color when we can have four, or six, for that matter? We're out there to create award-winning, stand-out work—why close ourselves to the options available in this age of limitless technology? We're armed with a stackful of Pantone swatchbooks and an infinite array of CMYK color combinations, waiting to be employed by our imaginations. Isn't more color the better way to captivate and impress our audiences? After all, don't our clients come to us for more than the unimaginative, quick and dirty, one-color results a quick copy shop can churn out "while-u-wait"?

But this, of course, is not the kind of one-color design this book is about. Our responsibility as visual communicators is to strive for higher standards in the face of the ubiquitous forces that would have us settle for the lowest common denominator. It is not our job to please everyone on the committee. We expect you will be inspired in the following pages by the ability of designers from all walks of life to push beyond preestablished views of what one-color design should be. As designing authors, we have sought to embody this in both the design of the book itself and the respectful presentation of the work we have selected to feature.

LET'S BE CLEAR. ONE-COLOR IS NOT:
Easier, instant, weak, restrictive, amateur, boring, simplistic, lukewarm, low-end.

ONE-COLOR IS:
Harder, striking, distinct, simple, memorable, rarely good, resourceful, intelligent—and oftentimes: ambitious, provocative, beautiful, edgy, jarring, witty, convicted, passionate.

In a world where so many forms of media vie for our attention—from our littered urban landscape of billboards to radio and television commercials surpassing ever-more over-the-edge tactics to wake us up out of our numbness just to remember a brand name or a number to "call now!"—it is imperative for us as creative people to strive for integrity in our work and to seek a higher standard for our craft.

It is our hope that this book becomes part of our industry's collective reach for excellence. We at Chen Design Associates were privileged to participate in this continuing dialogue by serving as jurors, authors, and designers of this book. To make our selections, our team exercised a rigorous system of judging over 1,000 submissions from around the world. We undertook an intense two-day process of critically considering each piece individually, voting silently, followed by in-depth group discussions for pieces that received mixed reviews. This open discussion became spirited at times, but allowed for some projects to be included that otherwise might have been overlooked. Our firm values collaboration and the strengths that each individual brings to the table, so this was an important part of our judging process.

Each selected piece was chosen because of its ingenuity, professionalism, and ability to demonstrate the power of design—with the central criterion of having used only one color on press. Non-ink processes such as emboss/deboss, blind hits, foil, die-cuts, and varnishes were acceptable, as were off-press ink techniques such as rubber stamping and laser printing. We divided the selected projects into the following five categories.

ORIGINS: THE CORE IDENTITY

These are pure presentations of corporate and organizational identities. How do you best capture the essence of what you are about in a single mark, or create a statement as captivating as possible in the dimensions of a business card, using only one color? The examples of identity systems and logos in this section demonstrate a cost-effective brilliance.

SCION: COLLATERAL OFFSPRING

This is the stuff that flows out of a foundational identity—everything from brochures and newsletters to marketing promotions and annual reports. These projects often have limited budgets. There is no lack of imagination here, however. Find out what can be done for a range of projects to arrest and engage an audience with just one color.

MACRO: DETAILS AT A DISTANCE

In this chapter we look at the large-scale impact of one-color designed posters, promotions, and other creative works for music, festivals, public service, health awareness, and theater. See what you never thought could be done with minimal ink at maximum size.

MICRO: AN INTIMATE IMPRESSION

We received so many stellar invitations and event pieces that we created a section just for them. There is something special about receiving a printed piece that speaks of quality and tactility. You view it up close, hold it in your hand, and are immediately involved with this small work of art.

VOLUME: THE THIRD DIMENSION

You've left the flat realm behind and entered the world of objects and packaging, books, music, fashion, and food. Can one-color have shelf presence in the marketplace? How does one-color design unify the complexities of volume and media other than paper and ink?

So run to it. Don't be scared of taking on that limited budget. Read on and be inspired. Let this book be a rejuvenating oasis for your mind and eye's imagination. And the next time that non-profit or small business you feel utterly passionate about has work to be done, attack the challenge of one-color with confidence. The creative possibilities (or limitations) are what you make them. You may very well discover that the best way to get your corporate client's message across is to reduce their vision of four-color, overproduced gloss to one-color, elegant uniqueness.

— Josh Chen and the Chen Design Associates team

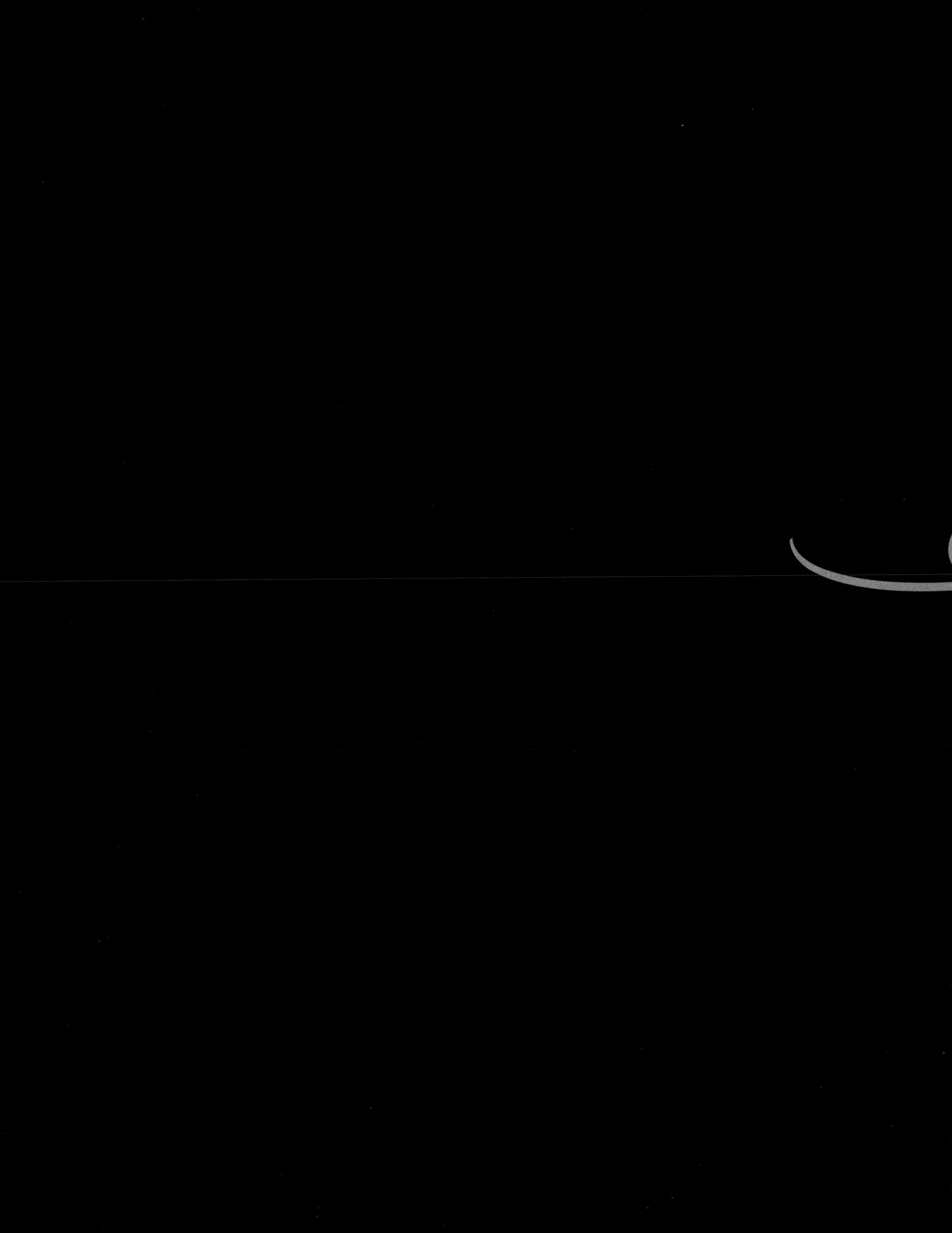

ORIGINS

THE CORE IDENTITY

letterhead / business card / envelope / logo

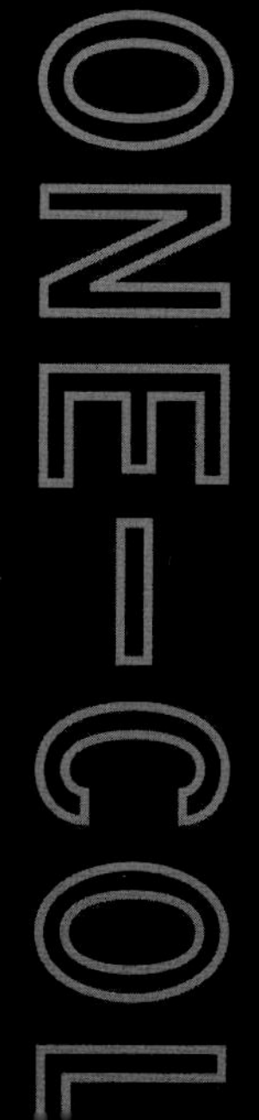

★★★A Day in May identity

A Day in May Design

CLIENT. A Day in May Design
ART DIRECTORS/DESIGNERS. Eve Billig, Lesley Hathaway

TOOLS. QuarkXPress, Illustrator
PAPER. Classic Crest
PRINTING. Full Circle Press

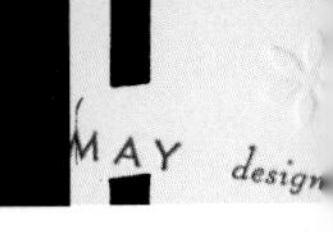

CLIENT. Jill Savini
ART DIRECTOR/DESIGNER. Jill Savini

TOOLS. Illustrator, Macintosh
PAPER. Crane's
PRINTING. Full Circle Press

***Savini Design identity

Savini Design

AGD Communications
395 Riverside Drive
New York, NY 10025

395 Riverside Drive New York, NY 10025 Tel 212.864.0000 Fax 212.663.3888
e-mail: ADee@agdcomm.com www.agdcomm.com

Alan Dee
AGD Communications, Inc.
395 Riverside Drive New York, NY 10025
Tel 212.864.0000 Fax 212.663.3888

Alan Dee
212.864.0000 Fax 212.663.3888
AGD Communications
395 Riverside Drive
New York, NY 10025
e-mail: ADee@agdcomm.com
www.agdcomm.com

AGD Communications, Inc.
395 Riverside Drive, New York, NY 10025

★★★Suzanne George identity

Elixir Design

CLIENT. Suzanne George
ART DIRECTOR. Jennifer Jerde
DESIGNERS. Jennifer Jerde, Holly Holmquist, Nathan Durrant
ILLUSTRATOR. Thomas Hennessy
PAPER. Fabriano, Crane's
PRINTING. Dickson's, Inc., Elizabeth Hubbell Studio

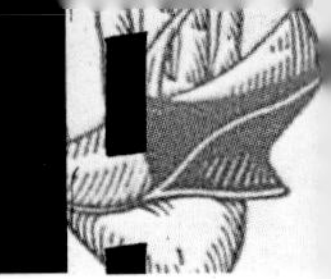

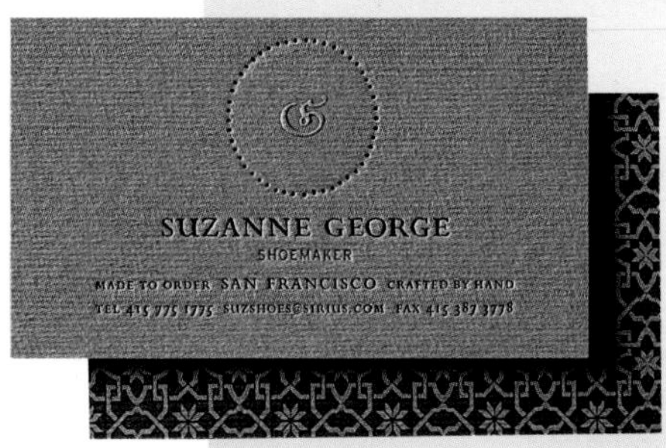

SUZANNE GEORGE
BETTY M
BROWN/WHITE
SUZANNE GEORGE
SHOEMAKER
SUZANNE GEORGE
SHOEMAKER
SUZANNE GEORGE
SHOEMAKER
SUZANNE GEORGE
SHOEMAKER
SUZANNE GEORGE
SHOEMAKER

★★★Freed Arnold Architecture identity

Nassar Design

CLIENT. Freed Arnold Architecture
ART DIRECTOR. Nelida Nassar
DESIGNER. Margarita Encomienda
TOOL. QuarkXPress
PAPER. Neenah UltraWhite, Curious
PRINTING. Offset

CLIENT. Tabu Nightclub
DESIGNER. Jeff Matz
TOOLS. Illustrator, QuarkXPress
PAPER. Classic Crest Solar White
PRINTING. Offset

★★★Art Center College of Design Alumni Council logo

Gee & Chung Design

CLIENT. Art Center College of Design Alumni Council
ART DIRECTOR/DESIGNER/ILLUSTRATOR. Earl Gee
TOOLS. Illustrator, Macintosh

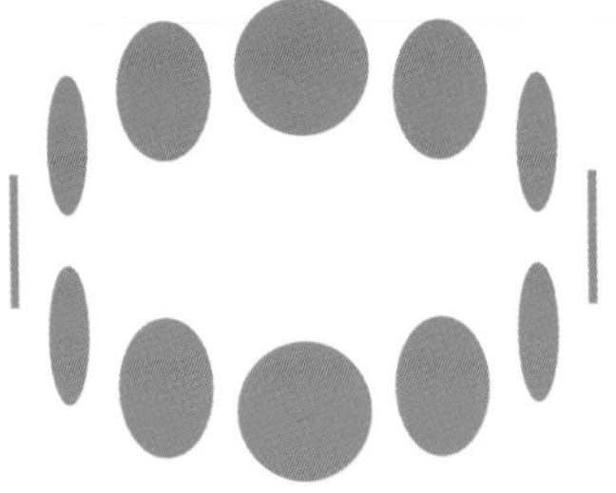

CLIENT. Jorge Silvetti
ART DIRECTOR/DESIGNER. Nelida Nassar

TOOLS. Hand typeset
PAPER. Crane Crest
PRINTING. Engraving

***Jorge Silvetti identity

Nassar Design

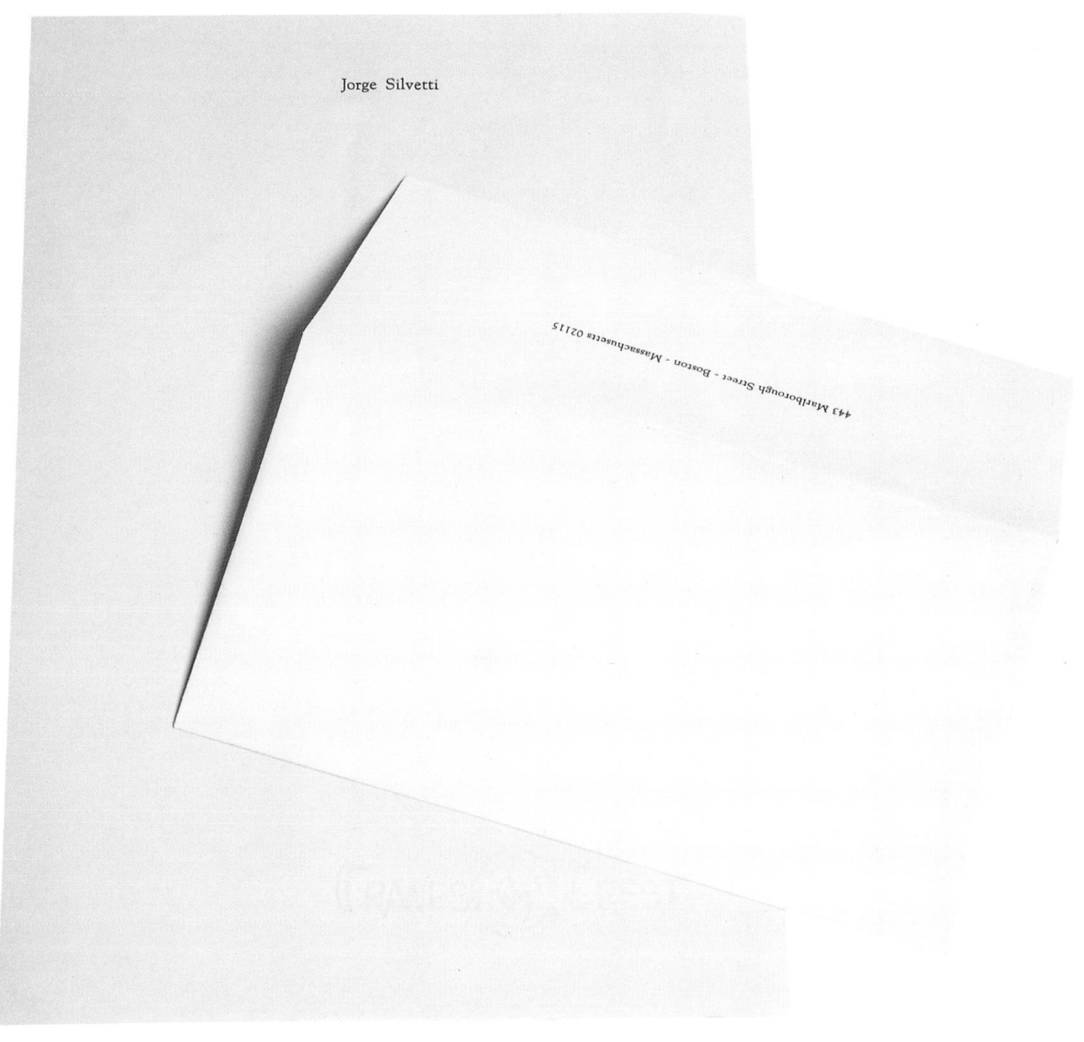

★★★High Watch Farm letterhead

Flux

CLIENT. High Watch Farm
ART DIRECTOR. Steve Barretto
DESIGNER. Leonardo Calderón
TOOLS. Illustrator, Macintosh

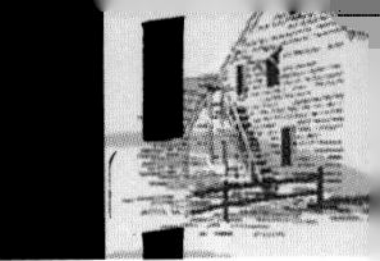

CLIENT. José J. Dias da S. Junior
DESIGNER. José J. Dias da S. Junior

TOOLS. Corel Draw, PC
PAPER. Color Plus
PRINTING. Offset silver

★★★Carnahan Landscape identity

Choplogic

CLIENT. Bruce Carnahan Landscape Design, Inc.
ART DIRECTOR/ILLUSTRATOR. Walter McCord
DESIGNERS. Walter McCord, Mary Cawein
TOOLS. QuarkXPress, Macintosh
PAPER. Mohawk Superfine
PRINTING. Offset lithography

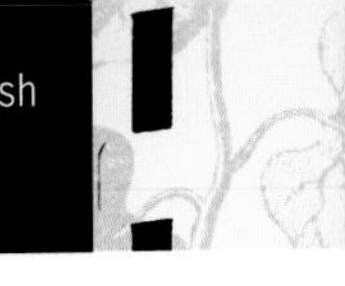

CLIENT. Elixir Design
ART DIRECTOR. Jennifer Jerde
DESIGNERS. Jennifer Jerde, Nathan Durrant
PAPER. Curious Popset
PRINTING. Dickson's, Inc.

VERIDICAL
REAL-TIME URBAN SIMULATION
VERIDICAL
REAL-TIME URBAN SIMULATION
VERIDICAL
REAL-TIME URBAN SIMULATION
RICK OLAUSON, DIRECTOR
MARKETING & SALES
RICK@VERIDICAL.COM
person
5338 N. MARINA PACIFICA DR.
LONG BEACH
CA 90803-7012
locale
VERIDICAL
REAL-TIME URBAN SIMULATION
TEL: 562.598.5888
FAX: 598.5881
WWW.VERIDICAL.COM
contact

CLIENT. Veridical
ART DIRECTOR. Bill Cahan
DESIGNER. Todd Simmons

TOOLS. Illustrator, QuarkXPress
PAPER. Neenah Classic Crest

★★★Veridical identity
Cahan & Associates

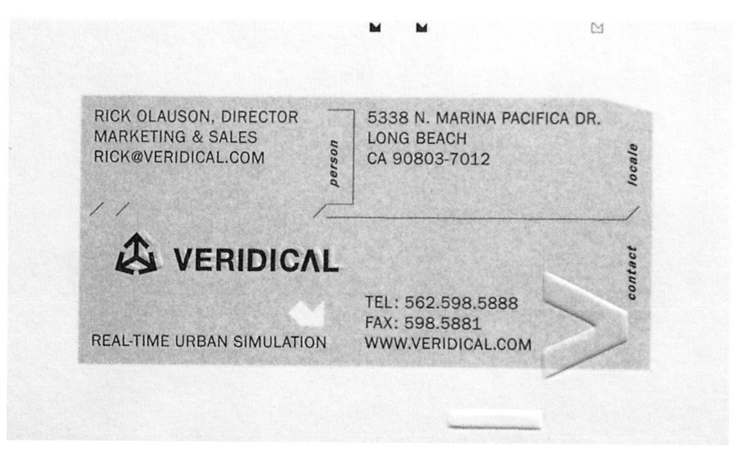

★★★Castor Henig identity

Elixir Design

CLIENT. Castor Henig Architecture
ART DIRECTOR. Jennifer Jerde
DESIGNERS. Holly Holmquist, Jennifer Jerde
PAPER. Fabriano (bcard), Crane's (ltrhd)
PRINTING. Dickson's, Inc.

CLIENT. Campion Wines
ART DIRECTOR. Tony Auston
DESIGNER. Don Whelan
ILLUSTRATOR. Mike Gray
TOOLS. Illustrator, Photoshop, Macintosh
PAPER. Mohawk Superfine Softwhite
PRINTING. Dickson's, Inc.

★★★2001 Dogwood Festival logo

Jeanne Macijowsky Design

CLIENT. 2001 Dogwood Festival
ART DIRECTOR/DESIGNER. Jeanne Macijowsky
TOOLS. Illustrator, Photoshop

CLIENT. Form Fünf
DESIGNERS. Ulysses Voelker, Daniel Bastian, Martin Veicht

TOOLS. QuarkXPress, Fontographer
PAPER. Gohrsmühle Bankpost 100g
PRINTING. Offset lithography

Daniel Henry Bastian
Kohlhökerstraße 53
D-28203 Bremen
form fünf
f5
Verbale und
visuelle
Kommunikation
Martin Veicht
Sommestraße 5
Telefon
Fax
Isdn
Düsseldorf
Bremen
Regensburg
Düsseldorf
Bremen
Regensburg
form fünf
f5
Verbale und
visuelle
Kommunikation
Jean Ulysses Voelker
Belsenstraße 4
40545 Düsseldorf
Telefon
0211 55 46 61
Fax
0211 55 46 15
Isdn
0211 55 46 61
mit besten Grüßen!
zur Korrektur!

Daniel Henry Bastian
Kohlhökerstraße 53
D-28203 Bremen
form fünf
mit besten Grüßen!

form fünf

form fünf
Alexanderstraße 98
D-28203 Bremen

***Knoll media kit

Decker Design

CLIENT. Knoll
ART DIRECTOR. Lynda Decker
DESIGNERS. Lynda Decker, Matt Hamlin

TOOLS. QuarkXPress, Illustrator
PAPER. Strathmore Pinstripe
PRINTING. Dickson's, Inc.

CLIENT. David Elinoff
ART DIRECTOR/DESIGNER. Aaron Cruse

MATERIALS. Glassine, 16-mm Film Leader, Player Piano Roll Paper
PRINTING. Silkscreen

***David Elinoff business cards

Dead Letter Type

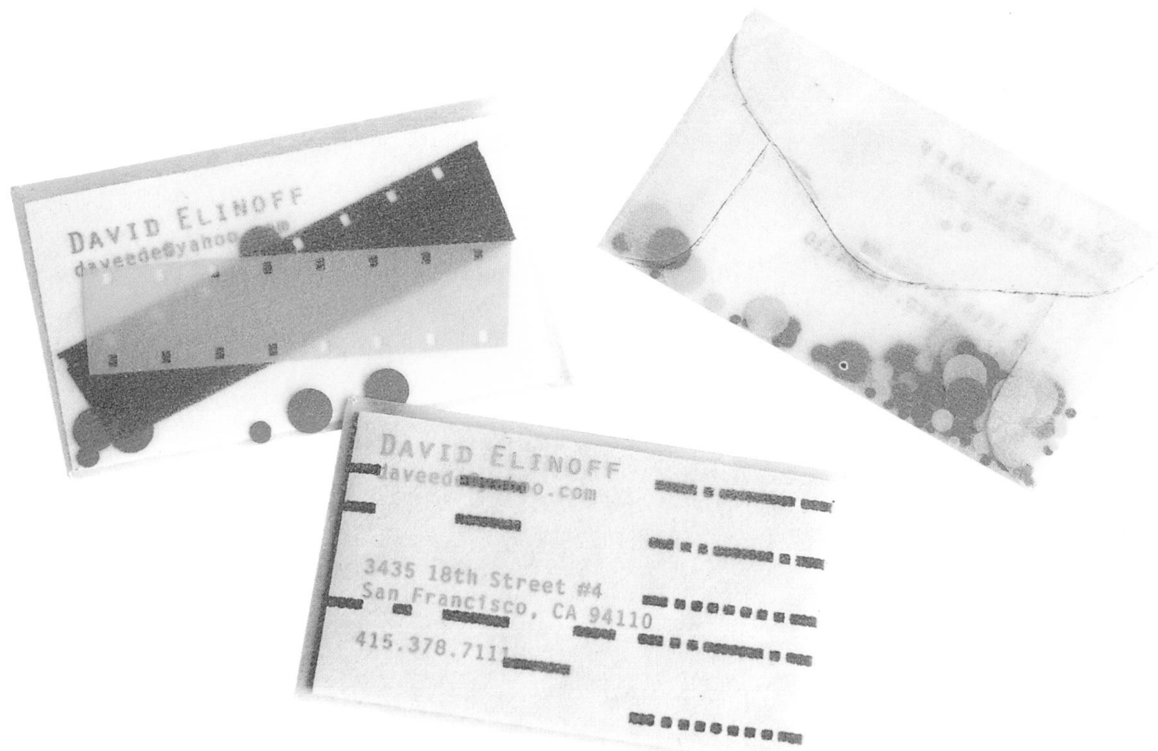

★★★EyeCandyTV.com biz card

Bløk Design

CLIENT. EyeCandyTV.com
ART DIRECTOR. Vanessa Eckstein
DESIGNERS. Vanessa Eckstein, Frances Chen

TOOLS. Illustrator, Macintosh
MATERIALS. Plastic, Chromatica Transparent, Strathmore
PRINTING. C.J. Graphics

CLIENT. Bowhaus Design Groupe
ART DIRECTOR/DESIGNER. Matt O'Rourke
TOOL. Illustrator

★★★Brophy identity

Drive Communications

CLIENT. Donna Lynn Brophy Photography
ART DIRECTOR. Michael Graziolo
DESIGNERS. Tim Goldman, Michael Graziolo

TOOLS. Illustrator, Photoshop, Macintosh
PAPER. Champion Carnival Yellow (text, cover)
PRINTING. Letterhead and postcard printed black. Red rubber stamp on all pieces.

CLIENT. Periwinkle Flowers
ART DIRECTORS. Scott Christie, Kevin Hoch
DESIGNERS. Scott Christie, Erin Boyce
ILLUSTRATOR. Emily Duvervilli
TOOLS. Photoshop, QuarkXPress, Macintosh
PAPER. Plainfield Bright White Smooth
PRINTING. McDougal & Pollard

★★★Periwinkle Flowers
business card

Pylon Design, Inc.

(FIT FOR A WALLET)

PERIWINKLE FLOWERS
1961 AVENUE ROAD, TORONTO, ONTARIO M5M 4A3
416.322.6985

★★★R. Seagraves identity

Elixir Design

CLIENT. Richard Seagraves
ART DIRECTOR. Jennifer Jerde
DESIGNER. Jennifer Tolo
PAPER. Crane's
PRINTING. Dickson's, Inc.

CLIENT. Chara Schreyer
ART DIRECTOR. Karin Myint
TOOL. Illustrator
PAPER. Crane's
PRINTING. Engraving and blind emboss

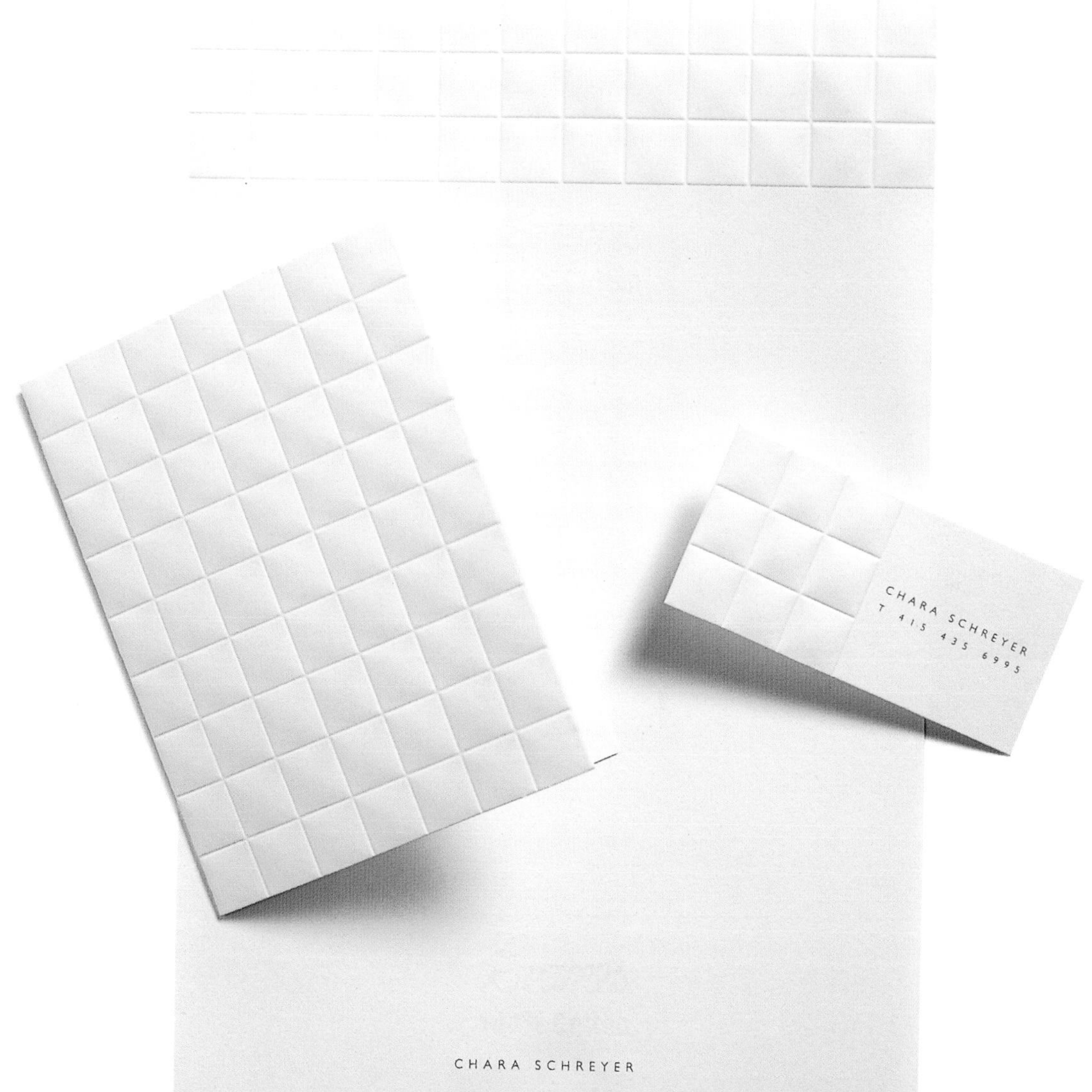

F R A M I N G A M Y

CLIENT. Amy Knapp
ART DIRECTOR/DESIGNER. Amy Knapp
TOOL. Illustrator

PAPER. Crane's Distaff Linen White Wove (ltrhd, eps); Crane's Pearl White with Beveled Silver Edges (bcard)
PRINTING. Full Circle Press

★★★Amy Knapp Design identity

Amy Knapp Design

SCION

COLLATERAL OFFSPRING

annual reports / brochures / magazines / campaigns / direct mail / promotions

***November 01 film calendar mailer

Flux

CLIENT. Yerba Buena Center for the Arts
ART DIRECTOR. Steve Barretto
DESIGNERS. Vanessa Dina-Barlow, Shilla Mehrafshani

TOOLS. QuarkXPress, Macintosh
PAPER. G-Print Matte Text
PRINTING. Trade Lithography

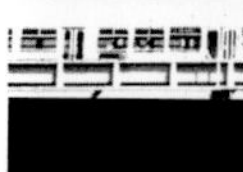

★★★December 01 film calendar mailer

Flux

CLIENT. Yerba Buena Center for the Arts
ART DIRECTOR. Steve Barretto
DESIGNERS. Vanessa Dina-Barlow, Shilla Mehrafshani
TOOLS. QuarkXPress, Macintosh
PAPER. G-Print Matte Text
PRINTING. Trade Lithography

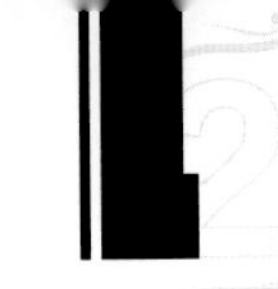

***Ballets Jazz de Montréal season brochure

KO Création

CLIENT. Ballets Jazz de Montréal
ART DIRECTOR/DESIGNER. Denis Dulude
PHOTOGRAPHERS. Pol Baril, Nicole Rivelli, Joël Dumoulin
TOOLS. Illustrator, Photoshop, QuarkXPress, Macintosh
PAPER. Conda Supreme
PRINTING. Sheet-fed offset

lumière espace temps

La salle et la scène sont plongées dans le noir pendant quelques instants. La réalité s'estompe, il n'y a plus d'espace, de temps, de lumière. Que votre souffle. D'un seul coup, vos sens sont interpellés, la lumière vous fait découvrir des corps dans cet espace déterminé par la scène et pourtant illimité, sans frontières, toujours renouvelé par l'imaginaire des créateurs, des artistes et des spectateurs. Pendant quelques battements de cœur, vous accompagnerez les danseurs dans leur univers qui deviendra aussi le vôtre. Le temps suspendra dans votre mémoire l'arabesque d'un bras, la lumière vous associera à son rythme, et l'espace confondra en une éphémère éternité l'artiste et le spectateur.

Puis, pendant quelques instants, la scène et la salle se replongeront dans le noir, vous vous lèverez de votre fauteuil, vous émergerez de cette rencontre unique, singulière et plurielle, et vous quitterez une réalité pour en rejoindre une autre ... peut-être la vôtre.

Louis Robitaille, directeur artistique

Texte/Text
Maryse Lapointe

Traduction/Translation
Charles Phillips

Light—Time—Open Space

For a few moments, darkness engulfs the stage and auditorium. Reality blurs; space, time and light vanish; only your breath remains. Suddenly your senses are summoned, and light reveals bodies moving in a space defined by the stage, yet unlimited, borderless, charged with the imagination of creators, artists and spectators. For a few heartbeats, you journey with the dancers into their universe, a world you now share. Time etches in your memory an arm in arabesque while light urges you to partake of its rhythm, and space merges artists and spectators in an ephemeral eternity.

Again, the stage and auditorium briefly plunge into darkness. You rise from your seat and emerge from a unique, multileveled encounter, leaving one reality, returning to another—perhaps your own.

Louis Robitaille, Artistic Director

La maîtresse de ballet ⁘ The Ballet Mistress

Hua Fang Zhang → Originaire de Shanghai, Hua Fang a été formée à l'Académie de danse de Pékin. Elle danse comme soliste du Ballet central de Chine, joint le Ballet de Hong Kong comme première danseuse, et en 1989 devient membre des BJM. En 1995, toujours danseuse au sein des BJM, elle est nommée maîtresse de ballet. Elle se consacre totalement à ses responsabilités de maîtresse de ballet depuis 1998.

Hua Fang Zhang → *Shanghai-born Hua Fang received her training at the Beijing Dance Academy. She performed as a soloist with the Central China Ballet, and as principal dancer with the Hong Kong Ballet. Her association with the BJM began in 1989. In 1995 while still a dancer with the BJM, she was appointed ballet mistress. Since 1998, she has concentrated exclusively on her new responsibilities.*

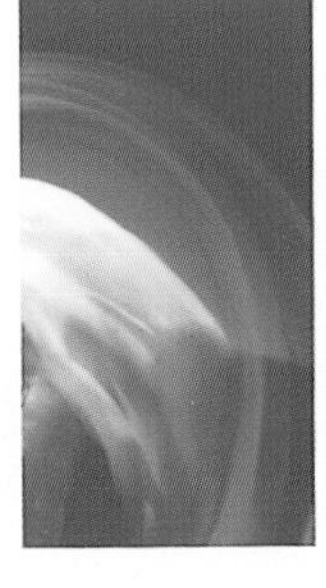

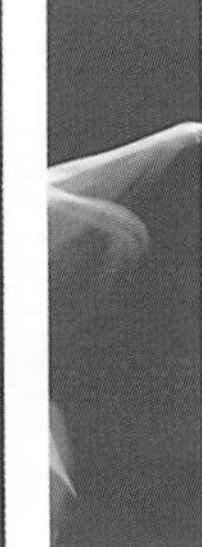

les BALLETS jazz de Montréal

ESPACE GO

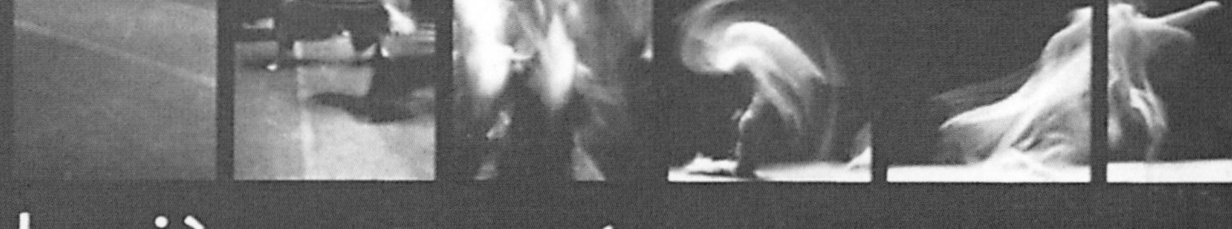

Directeur artistique
ouis Robitaille
Artistic Director

programme

lumière espace temps
Light–Time–Open Space

du 4 au 15 avril 2001
April 4 to 15 2001

2000 / 2001

TRENTE-HUITIÈME ASSEMBLÉE GÉNÉRALE ANNUELLE

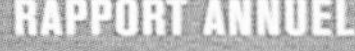

RAPPORT ANNUEL

2000–2001

Cinémathèque québécoise

/2001

RAPPORT D'ACTIVITÉS

FAITS SAILLANTS

IL A BEAUCOUP ÉTÉ QUESTION D'ARGENT À LA CINÉMATHÈQUE CETTE ANNÉE. JUSQUE SUR LA PLACE PUBLIQUE. LES FINANCES DE LA CINÉMATHÈQUE AURONT FAIT L'OBJET D'ARTICLES, D'OPINIONS ET MÊME DE PÉTITIONS.

LA CINÉMATHÈQUE QUÉBÉCOISE

MEMBRES DU CONSEIL D'ADMINISTRATION 2000-2001

Président
Jean Beaudry, réalisateur

Vice-présidents
Michel Murray, réalisateur
Kevin Tierney, producteur, Park Ex Pictures inc.

Secrétaire
Pierre Pageau, professeur de cinéma, Cégep Ahuntsic

Trésorier
*Paul Moreau**, vice-président exécutif, Les conseillers en management Maroco inc.

Administrateurs
*Michel Brault**, réalisateur et directeur de la photographie
Bernard Émond, réalisateur
Zénaïde Lussier, avocate
*René Malo***, président, Cinémalo inc.
*John R. Porter**, directeur, Musée du Québec
*Paul Racine***, président et chef de la direction, Canal Évasion
*Clément Richard***, avocat, président, Société de la Place des arts de Montréal
Hélène Roberge, réalisatrice et consultante en communication
Monique Simard, productrice, Productions Virage
*Hubert Stéphenne***, secrétaire et directeur général, Ordre des ingénieurs du Québec

MESSAGE DU PRÉSIDENT

Jean Beaudry

Robert Daudelin
Directeur général

Photo de la page couverture

3e trimestre 2001

CLIENT. Cinémathèque Québécoise
ART DIRECTOR/DESIGNER. Annie Lachapelle

TOOLS. QuarkXPress, Macintosh
PAPER. Bytonic by Spexel/Linen Vanilla
PRINTING. Sheet-fed offset

★★★Orchard Street Market collateral

Love Communications

CLIENT. Orchard Street Market
ART DIRECTOR. Preston Wood

DESIGNERS. Preston Wood, Amy Veach
ILLUSTRATOR. Scott Greer

TOOLS. Illustrator, QuarkXPress
PAPER. Kraft
PRINTING. DuMac

ORCHARD
STREET
MARKET
Where freshness is always in season.

ORCHARD
STREET
MARKET
Where freshness is
always in season.

54
C / G
CION

Where Freshness Is Always In Season
Large Vine Ripened Hot House Tomatos .99¢
English Hot House Cucumbers .99¢
Young Tender Green Broccoli .59¢
Large Tangerines .59¢
Huge! Premium Baking Potatoes .39¢
Curtell's Artisan Hubcap Italian Bread $149
Coke-Cola 6-packs $149
Squatters Beer $11.99
$4.99
Tony's Italian Pastry Pizza 3/$6.00
Premium #1 Jewel Yams 49¢ LB.
Snappy Red Radishes or Tangy Green Onions Mix or Match 4 for $1.00
ORCHARD STREET MARKET

Sweet Peaches.
Juicy Savings.
Sweet, juicy peaches are now in season. At Orchard Street Market, that means you can enjoy locally grown peaches oozing with flavor. Peaches ripened on the tree, not in a store. Delivered fresh from the orchards to our store every day. Treat your family to natural goodness of fresh, locally grown peaches. At a price that's just as sweet.
69¢ LB.
ORCHARD STREET MARKET
7070 South 2300 East • Salt Lake City, Utah 84121 • 801.455.1555

Free Sample!
We invite you to discover the flavor of a new kind of market, based on an old idea. We're a farmers' market.
And we'd like you to simply bring in this bag to Orchard Street Market, and fill it with whatever fresh produce you'd like. It's on the house: as in you won't pay anything.
We think you'll enjoy the farmers' market experience: where fruits and vegetables are gently picked and rushed to the market. (Along with the fresh dairy, deli, bakery and meat items we offer.)
Where freshness means everything. And where people greet you with a genuine smile and are happy to offer a free sample or even a tip or two.
That's us. Come by and sample how fresh produce can be.
ORCHARD STREET MARKET
Where Freshness Is Always In Season
OPEN REGULAR PICKERS' HOURS.
Seven Days a Week • Open 8 a.m. to 10 p.m.
11041 South Eastern • Henderson • 990-2770
Sample bag offer good 4/28/2000 to 5/8/2000

ORCHARD STREET MARKET
7070 South 2300 East
Suite #200
Salt Lake City, Utah 84121
801.455.1555
Fax: 801.455.9735

ORCHARD
STREET
MARKET
ORCHARD
STREET
MARKET
GRANNY SMITH

★★★The Operatic Era brochure

ALR Design

CLIENT. Target Margin Theater
ART DIRECTOR/DESIGNER. Noah Scalin
ILLUSTRATOR. David Zinn

TOOLS. QuarkXPress, Macintosh
PAPER. Domtar Weeds (text), Domtar Sandpiper (cover)
PRINTING. Offset

ARTIFACTS

This totemic artefact is one of our most exceptional finds. It appears to be a giant theic mask; a fertility god has been hypothesized.

Beaumarchais' classic contains evidence of radical revolution in the social order and bitter personal heartbreak. Yet joyous festivity in the secular sphere is also present; our team has identified numerous "jokes" as part of a so-called "comic tradition." We feel that this work can only be explained by a keen reversal of power structures amid celebration. But how are we to understand the resolution? This dig has been especially fascinating as a precursor to *Opera Mozartiana*.

ARTIFACTS

The revolutionary comedy that inspired Mozart's great opera. This classic of sexual intrigue and social power shook France in the 18th century, and it will shake New York in 2001.

The Marriage of Figaro

by Pierre Augustin Caron de Beaumarchais
Directed by David Herskovits

Emily Phillips, Scenery
Miranda Hoffman, Costumes
Josh Epstein, Lighting

At The Ohio Theater 66 Wooster Street
(see location a. on the Supplemental Information Map)

Previews start Oct. 10
Opening Oct. 17

Reservations 212-358-3657

THE DISCOVERY OF

The Operatic Era

"TARGET MARGIN THEATER GOES TO THE OPERA"

A SEASON OF THEATRICAL ARCHÆOLOGY AND CREATIVE SCIENCE
2001–2002

★★★Su-zen sale cards

Mucca Design

CLIENT. Su-zen
ART DIRECTOR. Matteo Bologna
DESIGNERS. Andrea Brown, Matteo Bologna
TOOLS. Freehand, Macintosh
PRINTING. Sioux Printing

★★★Identix 1999 Annual Report

Cahan & Associates

CLIENT. Identix
ART DIRECTOR. Bill Cahan
DESIGNER. Michael Braley

TOOLS. QuarkXPress, Macintosh
PAPER. 70# Topkote Dull (cover, text)
PRINTING. Lithographix

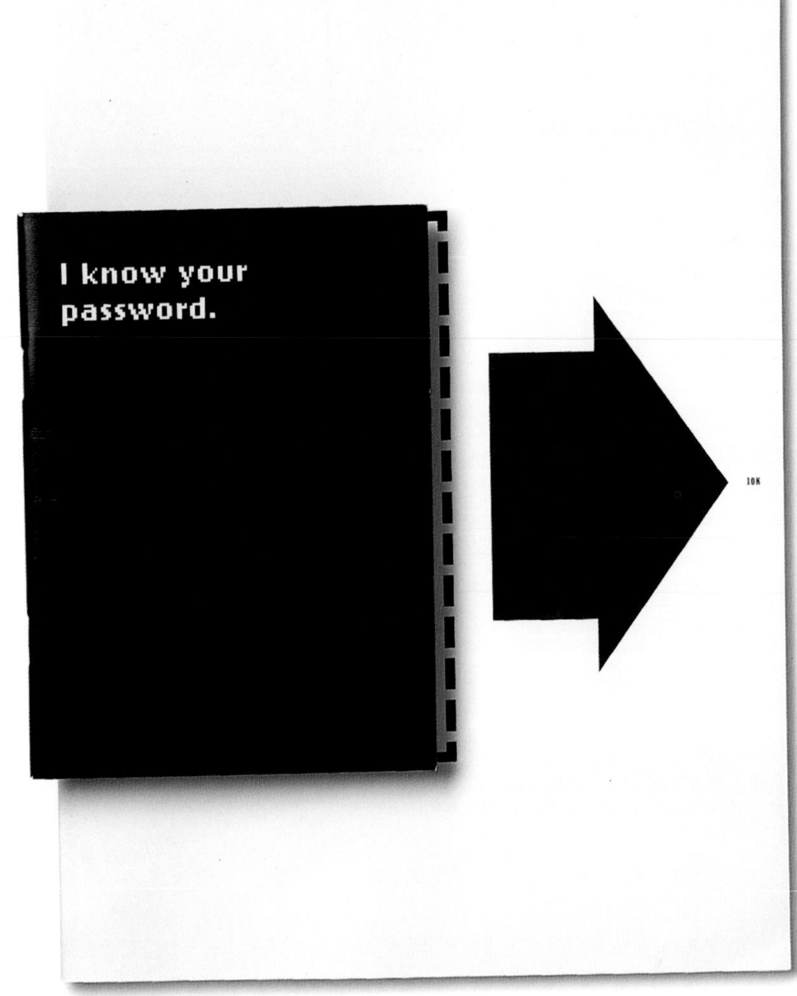

THE IDENTIX GOAL

To replace the overload of user ID cards, passwords, PINs, and other current authentication methods with something permanent and convenient that can never be forgotten, lost, stolen, forged or broken. Your fingerprint.

IDENTIX SCANS YOUR FINGERPRINT TO AUTHENTICATE YOU, AND ONLY YOU, FOR AUTHORIZED ACCESS AND TRANSACTIONS.

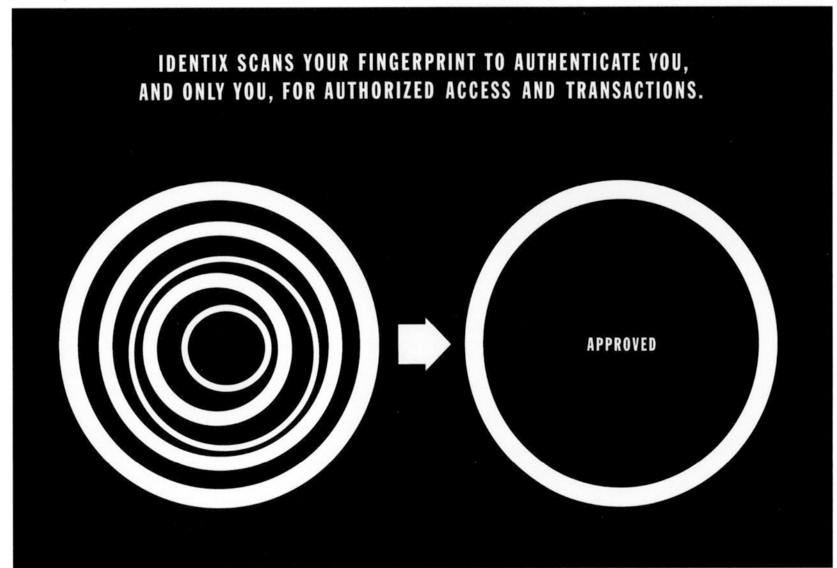

IDENTIX BIOMETRICS SOLUTIONS WILL BE INTEGRATED ACROSS ALL ENVIRONMENTS AND MARKETS...

E-COMMERCE

Biometrics will unlock the potential of e-commerce. Identix partners KeyTronic and Compaq provide fingerprint reader-equipped keyboards and peripheral devices, that will deliver high security for Internet transactions.

NETWORK AND SERVER ACCESS

Identix Biometrics enables the authorized user to access restricted networks, servers, databases, files and intranets with a single finger, eradicating password-related burdens on help desks.

BANKING AND FINANCIAL SERVICES

Through fingerprint authentication, Identix solutions make online transactions, account information and other banking and financial services more convenient and more secure.

DATABASE SECURITY

Identix fingerprint authentication prevents unauthorized database access and information theft. With BioLogon™, BioShield™ and BioSafe™, Identix can protect and encrypt information and applications.

FACILITY ACCESS

Identix physical access systems secure some of the most fortified sites, including military facilities. Identix's diverse installations range from armored cars to healthclubs.

AIRPORT SECURITY

Biometrics bolsters airport security and can deter terrorist activity. Chicago O'Hare International Airport uses Identix authentication for an array of security programs.

WIRELESS PHONES

Built-in fingerprint sensors will soon be an option for greater mobile phone security. Identix and Motorola have forged a partnership to build biometrics into wireless chip architecture.

***MFA in Writing ads

Aufuldish & Warinner

CLIENT. California College of Arts and Crafts

DESIGNER/PHOTOGRAPHER. Bob Aufuldish

TOOLS. Illustrator, Macintosh, Agfa DuoScan

***Frakcija magazine

Igor Masnjak Design

CLIENT. Frakcija, Performing Arts Magazine
ART DIRECTOR/DESIGNER/ILLUSTRATOR. Igor Masnjak

TOOLS. QuarkXPress, Photoshop, Freehand, Macintosh
PAPER. 135g/m^2 Magnomatt
PRINTING. Offset litho

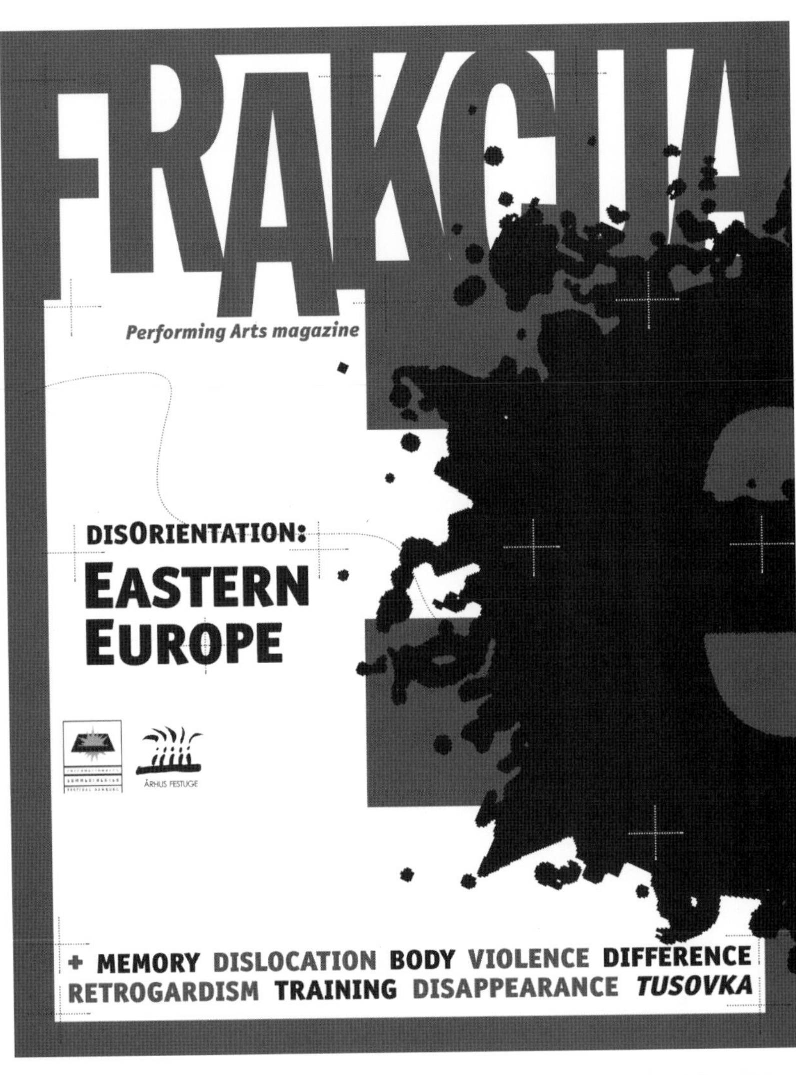

piše: Vladimir Stojsavljević

TJEDAN SUVREMENOG PLESA

PETNAEST GODINA

Festival **Mirne Žagar** kroz proteklih petnaest godina bilježio je istinske mijene suvremenog plesa i od zanimljive smotre prerastao je u međunarodnu manifestaciju o kojoj se danas govori i piše s ozbiljnošću i izvan Hrvatske.
Početak je bio pun entuzijazma i dogodio se 1984. godine. Program prvog Festivala sačinjavali su radovi mladih koreografa koji su tada činili zagrebački plesni krug. Ali već na drugom Festivalu postale su očitim ambicije i mogućnosti.
Stavljajući na program **Šparemblekov**, danas već legendarni, rad *Pjesme ljubavi i smrti* umjetnička voditeljica je svoj Festival pomaknula iz svijeta alternative u profesionalne vode. Na trećem Festivalu pojavili su se i prvi gosti iz Francuske, Austrije i Slovenije. Možda je najvažnije spomenuti da se prvi puta na Festivalu pojavio koreograf **Damir Zlatar Frey** s predstavom *Metastaze*. To je predstava urbanog senzibiliteta, istina ne još onako formiranog i umjetnički uobličenog kao što ćemo ga imati prilike gledati u predstavama drugih autora na idućim festivalima, ali za povijest ostaje činjenica da je to bio festivalski prvijenac ovog autora. Četvrti Tjedan suvremenog plesa prvi je opsežan i vrlo značajan po svojem programu.
Dolazak **Susanne Linke** (Njemačka) u Zagreb pamti se još i danas. Radi se o autorici istančanih ideja koje na pozornici pokazuje kao kombinaciju plesnog pokreta, tišine, mimske radnje i odnosa spram objekta. Njezino povlačenje kade po pozornici Gavelle u najmanju ruku je zauvijek slomilo predrasudu o plesnoj umjetnosti kao visokoformalnoj i lijepoj zabavi. Drugi nastup Damira Zlatara Freya na Festivalu s predstavom *Raspeće Glorije*, u izvedbi ZPA, pokazao je koliko su elementi koreodrame ušli na domaću scenu, i ne samo radi Freyevih intimnih preokupacija nego i zbog plesačkih mogućnosti sudionica predstave. I prisutnost **Jasne Knez** na ovom Festivalu svakako je od važnosti za povijest jer je prva pokazala pretapanje konceptualnosti i plesnog izričaja koji danas ima svoje snažne predstavnike, primjerice **Truus Bronkhorst** iz Nizozemske. Koliko tehnika može plesača odmaknuti od baleta i vinuti ga do neslućenih izražajnosti vidjelo se u predstavi kultne grupe **Diversions** iz Engleske.
Peti Festival bio je sasvim legitiman međunarodni Festival, na kojem su dva autora pokazala sve ono o čemu su već nastale knjige u kojima se dramskog glumca i plesača opisuje kao idealnu sintezu imenovanu — izvođač.
Naime, **Joseph Nadj** pokazao je svoju predstavu *Sedam nosorogovih koža* koja je oduševila gledalište, ali i kritiku i profesionalce. Nadj danas ima svoje kazalište i svoj stil, ali 1988. godine prvi susret s njim na ovom Festivalu pokrenuo je niz teorijskih pitanja. U njegovoj predstavi smo prvi puta vidjeli na koji način se koristi iskustvo borilačkih istočnjačkih vještina, kako se stvara danas već legalizirana dramaturgija u plesnoj predstavi (funkcija dramaturga je i dandanas za naše cjelokupno glumište preuranjena inovacija), kako se postiže scenska apstrakcija s običnim predmetima poput stolca te ulogu humora unutar ozbiljnih tema kao kontrapunkt.

Truus Bronkhorst

Drugi autor koji je nezaobilazan kad govorimo o 5. Tjednu suvremenog plesa je danas već pokojni **Larry Leong**, čijim smo predstavama *Eventides* i *Dark Light* vidjeli fascinantnu koncentraciju izvođača koja se postiže zahvaljujući istočnjačkim vještinama i upotrebu tišine u plesnoj predstavi kao dramskog naboja.
Na 6. Tjednu suvremenog plesa prvi put se pojavio **Matjaž Farič** sa svojim istočnim plesnim projektom i predstavom *Rdeči alarm* gdje je na nevjerojatan način predvidio onu budućnost bivše države, njezin rasap, koju smo doživjeli svega dvije godine kasnije. Ova predstava je važna i zbog toga što dokumentira koliko se plesna umjetnost približila

Elisa Monte Dance Company

42 FRAKCIJA

43

FRAKCIJE

Zagrebačko kazalište mladih
Zagrebački plesni ansambl
Lanonima Imperial
J.C. Garcia:
Prepoznavanje krajolika

Teatar Exit
Zagrebačko kazalište mladih
N. Lušetić:
Žudnja

ČEGA TO KRAJOLIK?

Piše: Goran Sergej Pristaš

Prije nekog vremena jedan me je kolega, stranac, pitao kako je živjeti u "prostoru nevolja" ("trouble area" moglo bi se prevesti i kao problematično područje, ali taj kontekst neka se odnosi više na nekoga tko živi izvan mišljenog prostora i tiče ga se prostor kao problematičan, a ne nevolje koje s njim dijele isti prostor) i koliko su te nevolje prisutne u mom svakodnevnom životu. Lako je bilo voditi razgovor - kolega je mislio na Zagreb, Hrvatsku, ove tu prostore... i? Razmišljajući kasnije o tom pitanju provjeravao sam u sebi koji bi to točno bio prostor. Zamislio sam ga, valjda, kao prostor koji dijelim s drugim ljudima i stvarima, koji me aficiraju tako da neka njihova djelovanja i odnosi u koje stupam s njima smatram lošim, nevoljom. Takvo određenje primjenjivo je na svakodnevne ljudske susrete, svakodnevne sudare s onim što čini *loše* u odnosu na neko drugo *dobro*. Prostor nevolje, dakle, određuje prostornost stvari s kojima se nekome događa nešto loše u odnosu na nešto drugo što je bilo bolje. Kratko i jasno: nevolje su bile ratne.
Znajući da me je taj kolega pitao o nevoljama koje je donio rat, pokušao sam pobrojati ne ono što je *loše*, a što je donio art, nego ono *dobro*, u odnosu na koje je to *loše* upravo takvo. I tu se slika počinje raspadati. Krenem li od bilo kojeg dobrog, pokaže se da je ono bilo *loše* po neko drugo *dobro* prije toga. A ta ista *dobra* su se prometala brzo (na ovim zemljopisnim područjima možda brže nego drugdje) u *loše*. Nije trebalo dugo da shvatim da uzročno-posljedična konstrukcija, ona koja bi ispričala priču bilo koje nevolje, ne vodi nikamo jer ni jedna od tih priča nije dostatna da bi pružila uvid u prostor ni u moje vlastite nevolje, a kamoli nekakav opći prostor nevolje. Taj prostor se onda čini jasnijim izvana negoli iznutra jer ne uvjetuje promjenu stanja onoga tko ga misli, nego aficira utoliko da stvara predodžbu cjeline.
Raspadnut u detaljima naših pojedinačnih života, sudbina, tragedija, smrti, klanja, pobjeda, gubitaka i ideja, isti prostor postao je nesaglediv i svaka želja u nama da ga sagledamo pretvara se u čistu kartografiju. *Pejsaž* nam je nestao iz vidokruga. Tu i tamo javi se nostalgija za *predodžbama* koje smo imali želeći prostor (zemlju), ovakav ili onakav. Priče naših nevolja su priče pojedinačnih želja i razočaranja. A žrtve naših želja skrivene su ispod kartografije. Duboko da se ne vide. Zajedno s nekim drugim željama nekih ljudi prije nas, pretvorile su se u svoje suprotnosti koje logika moći nameće.
Ukoliko želim stvari gledati kartografski, mnogo je toga jasnije. Tada i divljanje dobrog i lošeg postaje ukroćeno jer na karti je ispisano Dobro i Zlo. Paradoksalno je koliko nedetaljna karta, karta u mijenjanju, slika koja predočava prostor, koja reducira bitno da bi pokazala "bitno" izgleda uvjerljivije i jasnije od krajolika, stvarnog prostora u kome postoji sve bitno. Moj je spomenuti kolega, vjerojatno, pažljivo gledao televiziju, *izvještaje s Balkana* i "stekao potpuni uvid u to što se ovdje događa". Taj je pak uvid daleko detaljniji i od logike kartografije. Logika kartografije brutalna je

Foto: Nino Šolić

6 FRAKCIJA

FRAKCIJA 7

BRECHT 8

KA MATERIJALISTIČKOM KAZALIŠTU

Nešto je trulo
u državi Danskoj.
W. Shakespeare,
Hamlet

Nešto je trulo
u ovom vremenu nade.
H. Müller,
Hamletmašina

Cijeli je Sečuan
običan kup govana.
B. Brecht,
Dobar čovjek iz Sečuana

piše: **Aldo Milohnić**

Je li **Brecht** (još uvijek) "naš suvremenik"? Vrijedi li ga još igrati ili bismo trebali uzeti za ozbiljno izjavu nekadašnjeg Brechtovog učenika **Heinera Müllera**, koji je u, recimo, "trenutku slabosti" ustvrdio da možemo zaboraviti na cijeli Brechtov opus i kao jedinog aduta zadržati tek njegov nedovršeni tekst o Fatzeru? Zar doista jedan fragment može prevagnuti nad cijelim opusom jednog od najvećih i najplodnijih dramatičara dvadesetog stoljeća? I nadalje, ako ipak ta smjela Müllerova tvrdnja ne stoji, kako onda objasniti pad interesa za uprizorenja Brechtovih tekstova u npr. slovenskim kazalištima (zbog nedovoljne obaviještenosti, to se ne usuđujem tvrditi i za repertoare hrvatskih kazališta, premda pretpostavljam da u Hrvatskoj Brecht trenutno ne kotira ništa bolje negoli u Sloveniji)? Ili su nam možda od Brechta, toga klasika "našeg" stoljeća, ipak bliži klasici prijašnjih stoljeća?

Jan Kott je svojom knjigom *Shakespeare naš suvremenik* izazvao pravu pomutnju u teoretskom mastodontu zvanom "shakespeareologija". Ali zbunio je Kott ne samo autore shakespeareoloških studija, već i režisere, koji su tih godina (knjiga je prvi puta tiskana 1965. godine u Varšavi) suvremenost velikog elizabetinca često čitali kroz puke vizualije. Za Kotta Shakespeareova suvremenost nije bila u tome da režiser (ili kostimograf) Hamletu navuče traperice, već imanentna političnost njegovih drama. Suvremenost area je Kott prepoznao u uvijek aktualnom, "transhistorijskom" vrtuljku "Velikog Mehanizma", koji kraljeve, tirane, političare i ine vlastodršce uspinje na okrvavljeni prijestol (što mu nije mogao oprostiti **György Lukács**, jedan od prvih pomnih čitalaca njemačkog izdanja Kottove knjige, jer je po njegovom mišljenju Kott izbjegao historizirati Shakespearea). Pa ipak, nakon te znamenite i danas već klasične knjige, nitko se više nije usudio reći da je Shakespeare zastarjeo ili da više nema što reći našem vremenu, da recimo ne postavlja pitanja, koja bi bila relevantna za, kako kaže Brecht, "publiku koja zaista danas privređuje današnji novac i danas jede današnju govedinu".

U kazališnom programu, koji će biti tiskan uz jedno skorašnje uprizorenje **Molièreovog** Tartuffa u Sloveniji, trebao bi izaći i esej **Rastka Močnika** *Što je Molière nama, što smo mi Molièreu?* U tom tekstu, kojega sam imao priliku pročitati u rukopisu (pa dakle ne mogu tvrditi da do objavljivanja možda neće doživjeti i neke preinake), Močnik tvrdi da "kako se čini, Molièrea suvremenika treba tražiti na sceni, u ukroćenom međuprostoru između kanoničkog teksta europske kulture i ubitačnog prostaštva europske svakodnevice". Sva ta "klasicistička šara" (šeširi, perike, svilene čarape, klanjanje...)

Berliner Ensemble, Nezaustavljivi uspon Artura Uia, Režija: H.Müller

FRAKCIJE

Metafora javnosti

Tjedan performansa "Javno tijelo"; Zagreb, 14.-18. 10. 1997.

piše: **Suzana Marjanić**
snimio: **Boris Cvjetanović**

Josette Féral manipulaciju kojom performans podvrgava tijelo izvođača (performera) određuje *kameleonskim tijelom* (1996:208), i iz navedenoga ontologema tijela postavlja dodirnost između performansa i smrti: "*Performans* je kao fenomen djelovao kroz želju za smrću", a polazi od iskustva "tijela koje se ranjava, sakati i reže (...), tijela koje u potpunosti prihvaća *lesionizam*" (1996:209). I dok je, primjerice, **Ron Athey** na Eurokazu 1997. godine predstavom *Deliverance*[1] objavio vlastito tijelo "oljušteno" do srži, u kojemu je upisan tekst života suočavanja s vlastitom Smrću, a u predstavi *Incorruptible Flesh* (**Lawrence Steger** & Ron Athey) tijelo arhaične formule hermetičkog "ženomuža" (ženi sličan svetac) – muško spolovilo tehnikom "klamanja"-*piercing* metamorfozirano je u usjeklinu ženskoga spolovila, postavljajući u dodirnost *body art2* s formama ritualne tanatomorfoze i pročišćenja; *Tjedan performansa* pod nazivom *Javno tijelo*, u organizaciji zagrebačkoga Soros centra za suvremenu umjetnost (SCCA-Zagreb) i nezavisnog umjetničkog projekta *Doma-A casa-At Home*, koji je održan u Zagrebu 14-18. listopada 1997. godine, svojom radnom naslovnom sintagmom eksteriorizirao je privatno tijelo u *metaforu javnosti*.

1 usp. "Moderni primitivac" [illegible] Frakcija 1997:6, str. 62-65.
2 O [illegible] termina *body art* usp. [illegible] 1988:153.

Kameleonsko tijelo i tijelo kao otisak sjećanja (autobiografsko tijelo)

Razgovor s **Tomislavom Gotovcem** prigodom njegova performansa *Prilagođavanje objektima na Trgu maršala Tita (Trg maršala Tita, volim Te!)*

F *Kao uvodni okvir nekih svojih performansa odabrali ste podne (sat kada nema sjene) kao znak koji ih postavlja u dodirnost sa zbiljom, pa tako i za Podnevni performans.*

T. Gotovac: Isto je bilo podne kada sam izvodio *Ležanje gol na asfaltu, ljubljenje asfalta (Zagreb, volim te), Hommage to Howard Hawks' Hatari* (13. XI. 1981., petak, 12:00- 12:07 h, op. S. M.), isto je bilo podne prigodom otvaranja 10. muzičkog biennala 1979. godine. Mnogo svojih performansa na javnim prostorima obilježio sam znakom topa s Griča. Već su se stari Zagrepčani pobrinuli da označe prijelaz jednog dijela dana u drugi, tj. podne, znakom topa s Griča. A i taj pucanj s Griča je neka vrsta zvučnog simbola centra grada. Za vrijeme rata pojačali su dozu baruta tako da je top postao glasniji. A kako živim i radim u Zagrebu, kako se tu događaju sve moje životne manifestacije, onda volim da mi grad Zagreb daje znak za početak. Između ostalog, nitko dosad još nije upotrijebio taj top u smislu da mu on *komandira* početak. Međutim, ovaj *Podnevni performans* – kako su ga nazvali organizatori – to je bilo zato što nisam rekao kako će se zvati, ali pravi naziv performansa je *Prilagođavanje objektima na Trgu maršala Tita*. Kako je u akciji *Ležanje gol na asfaltu, ljubljenje asfalta (Zagreb, volim te)* – tu je *Trg maršala Tita, volim te.*

F *Simboličkim kružnim (i profilaktičkim)3 putovanjem u performansu kao uvodni i završni okvir označili ste Meštrovićev Zdenac života. Što je Meštrovićev Zdenac života Vama, a Vaš performans Zdencu života?*

T. Gotovac: Trg maršala Tita je vrlo značajan. Kada sam ga upoznao, u vrijeme NDH – kada sam došao u Zagreb 1941. godine, mislim da se zvao Trg Adolfa Hitlera. Prije toga, za vrijeme stare Jugoslavije, zvao se Trg kralja Aleksandra, a nakon rata preimenovan je u Trg maršala Tita. *Zdenac života* je prvo veliko umjetničko djelo koje sam kao klinac od četiri godine vidio kad sam došao u Zagreb. *Zdenac života* i ona rotonda su sastavni dijelovi moga djetinjstva. Isto tako i Kazalište i *Sveti Juraj* i Leksikografski zavod i Pravni faks, Kavkaz... čitav taj Trg su

3 Kružno kretanje Tomislava Gotovca oko "intermedije" urbane Trga maršala Tita može se interpretirati i u kontekstu profilaktičke magije, kao stvaranje zbranbenog pojasa oko Trga koji prediciraju autobiografske zapise, sjećanja.

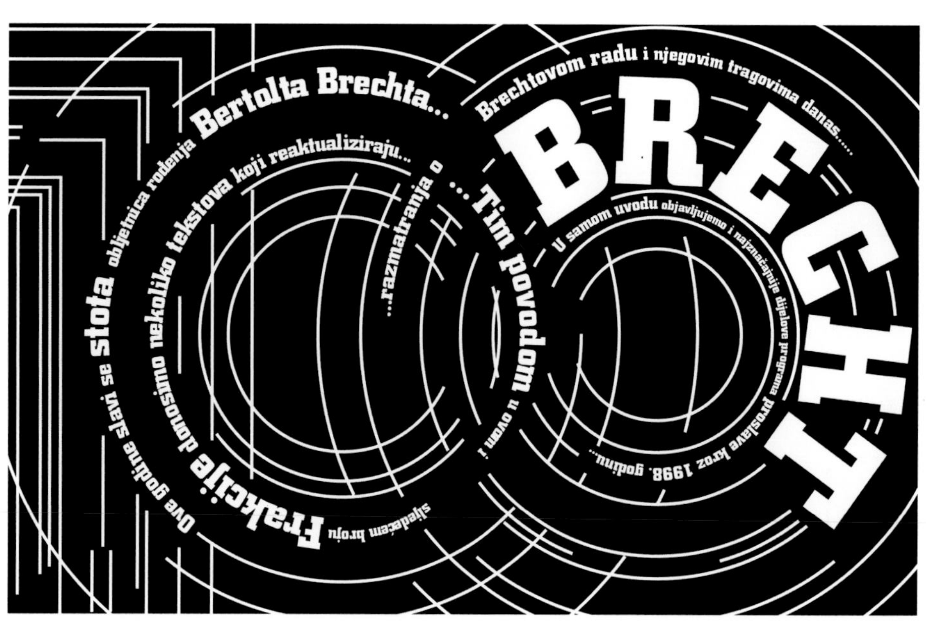
Ove godine slavi se stota obljetnica rođenja Bertolta Brechta...
Frakcije donosimo nekoliko tekstova koji reaktualiziraju...
sljedećem broju
...razmatranja o ...Tim povodom u ovom i
Brechtovom radu i njegovim tragovima danas.....
BRECHT
U samom uvodu objavljujemo i najznačajnije dijelove programa proslave kroz 1998. godinu...

Bojana Kunst

Of Body Natural and Artificial

In this essay I would like to go back a while, to the beginning of the century, and speak of one of the main characteristics of the then current utopias of the body, which have profoundly affected the representation of the body in the century now drawing to its close. The paradoxes, hidden in the utopias of the natural body, to this day continue to haunt and shape the fugitive margin of the body; the body, having already been through all imaginable forms of restructuring, deforming, deconstruction, as well as the innumerable ways of reading, appears now only as a scandal, always ready to point to the flesh (we can call it pleasure too), always coming in through the back door, always on that ever thinning line separating body from machine, at the moment, in the words of Donna Harraway, when "machines become disturbingly alive." A notion, dating from the early 20th century, seems to me to be typical of the thinking about utopias inscribed in the body, which also guard and dictate the ways of its representation: it is the hopeless search for the natural body, that after all determines the beginnings of modern dance also, as well as certain important shifts in theatrical representation. Movement is the representational strategy which has become the be-all and end-all of that search. Movement of any kind: "This new irrational 'something,' that comes from the flowing life flow, is the new corporeality... body culture, gymnastics, dance, cult dance, spatial dance, new corporeality, new bodily sensation, body-soul, new callisthenics, movement, rhythmics with its innumerable attributes... These are the signs of the new."[1] Movement as the basic method of naturalising and shaping of the body is the theme treated by some of the most eminent apologists of the return to the natural body, among them the most active and representative being the *Life Reform Movement* (*Lebensreformierung* or *Lebensreform-Bewegung*), which has explicitly combined the populist tendency for life and social reform of the masses with the aesthetic reform, and thus in the best tradition of the early 20th century movements, which have mostly sought to unite art and life, brought about the new concept of the body. Numerous pioneers of modern dance, e.g. Isadora Duncan, Ruth St. Denis, Ted Shawn, Mary Wigman, Rudolf Laban, who emphasised the return to the natural body, i.e. its autonomous expressivity, as the basic method of liberating modern dance from the traditional discourses (above all, the figural rhetoric of the ballet), were directly or indirectly involved with these movements. Aesthetic autonomy of the body has thus through *Lebensreformiernung* and through modern dance been developed above all by means of methodical exploration of the kinetics, i.e. the rhythmical quality, of the body, and through the real emancipational aesthetic theory of movement expression, that should bring man and his body back to their original being.

1 Wolfgang Graeser: *Körpersinn*, München, 1921.

When we inspect closely the character of the natural body in the statements of its apologists at the beginning of the 20th century, we should by no means be mislead by their enthusiasm, for it is easy to dismiss them at first sight as being only an expression of the resistance to industrialisation and the modern way of life. Although this resistance can be understood as the source of the important beginning-of-the-century movements, which somehow start to intimate the problematic co-existence of man and machine in the modern urban way of life, it is precisely in their techniques (that range from the search for rhythm and new kinetic structures, to such absurdities as nude skiing), that the fugitive, dynamic, energetic and kinetic body, that has no fixed skin boundary, is reflected, the body capable of endless kinetic flow, repetition, energetic efficiency, swaying, kinetic transmission and mediation: the body, then, the kinetic characteristics of which mirror the characteristics of modern motors, i.e. technological structures, confronting at the beginning of the century the human body with new forms of representation (the invisible dynamics of electricity, audio-visual machines, the problem of speed, etc.). Modern sports, dance, gymnastics, rhythmics, swimming, movement flow (occasionally accompanied by the use of other body codes), give back to the body some of its natural characteristics, simultaneously blending it with the actions of machines, training it to the new dynamic rhythm of automatised efficiency. The concept of natural body at the beginning of the century is thus not some new romantic concept of longing for nature, i.e. the natural life of the body, as it might at first seem; that body is in fact the body of hygienic minimum, obviously healthy and fertile body, the transformed body that has no problems in inhabiting some *machine habiter* of Le Corbusier's, in its essence already transformed and connected to the artificial. A blasphemous thought easily comes to mind, revealing the utopia constantly being disclosed in the case of the natural body: the image of body fullness, the techniques of representation of which are often caught in the image of the artificial, the automaton, the machine (this goes especially for the performing arts). The image, where the in fact impossible body - in this instance, the body of hygienic minimum, the body stripped of everything, presented as the sovereignty of kinetic flow only - is linked to the image of the machine, of artificial structure, hides in itself also the end of one of the most important utopias of the Enlightenment project, that at the beginning of the 20th century completely blends the natural and the artificial. No wonder, than, it was precisely the artificial body that in the thirties became the central metaphor which witnesses the wonder of life (of this I will say more in the conclusion).

What consequences does this have for the self-representation of the body? The emergence of modern dance is of special interest here, for a new artistic form was being born, the form which seems to reflect in its beginnings certain basic relations between the natural and the artificial. A fundamental insight seems to be the origin of modern dance: *expressive autonomy*, i.e. *kinetic autonomy*, of the body, which represents the body itself as an autonomous aesthetic field, subject only to its own epidermal openness and its own kinetic flow. Dance thus, in the words of the poet Val(ry, becomes "a way of inner life, which satisfies that psychological notion of new life, where physiology is dominant."[2] Although in almost every programmatic statement made by the reformers and originators of modern dance the tendency of return to the natural body is being emphasised,[3] sometimes also connected to the original ritual body, it is precisely in this tendency that we find the new physiology inscribed, the new body engineering, shaped in the collective co-existence of body and machine as the dynamic motor and kinetic energy structure, offering also the ideal of autonomy and power. The most important metaphors that we find in the artistic concepts in the beginnings of modern dance (and in everyday life too), like the movement flow (the key word when the expression of the body is to be designated), rhythmics, energy, rhythmic flow, thrusts, pulsations, swaying, etc. are, although understood as the basic means of making the body natural and free, in fact, characteristics of the body as dynamic motor. The union of body and machine in everyday urban way of life thus strongly influences the modern dance image of the body as pulsating movement flow. Every return to the origin of the body (in dance as well) is therefore paradoxically linked to it artificial/impossible equivalent.

2 Paul Valéry: "Philosophie de la danse" in: *Oeuvres I*, Editions Gallimard, 1957, p. 1390.

3 Cf. Isadora Duncan in her book *The Dancer of the Future*. Also: "For hours I would stand quite still, my two hands folded between my breasts, covering the solar plexus (...) I was seeking, and finally discovered, the central spring of all movement." Isadora Duncan: *My Life*, London: Victor Gollancz Ltd., 1928, p. 84; New York, Liverlight, 1927, p. 75.

It would be wrong to understand the aforementioned as a process that, despite certain illusions of returning to its origins, deprives the body of its autonomy and subjects it to the artificial. It is important that, through revealing some links between the natural and the artificial, we can follow certain characteristics of new bodily representation. All the more, it seems, because this interplay of body and machine (i.e. the characteristics of new technology), gives back its autonomy to the body, not only establishing it as a new autonomous aesthetic form with a specific system of signs and a separate structure, but turning its autonomous expressivity into the fundamental system of meaning in modern dance, the fugitive kinetics into its structural network, a form no longer mimetic but dynamic and subject to its own laws. And this autonomy is specific, determined by the fugitive quality and dynamics of the artificial structure, the comprehensibility of the sign no longer being its concern. Herein lies the essential paradox of movement as the basic technique of making the body natural: it draws attention to the body, although it is losing it ever more, the moving body becoming a loose structural network, a minimalist play of parts, shadows, traces. The meaning, therefore, vanishes, and in its stead a "structure" is revealed, which later also becomes the essential modernist paragon and model of the existence of the body.

The French philosopher Michel Bernard claims that one of the consequences of the new physicality of the body is precisely the precedence of energy over meaning, which results in the breakdown of communication, i.e. in the reception becoming more difficult.[4] Instead of a transparent gestural body sign, we have in front of us a pulsating energy field: the expressivity of the body equals the epidermal energy flow. Thus the very structural and representational status of the body is changed, the new kinetic body refuses to be subjected to the imperialism of the transparent sign and instead of it declares the sovereign intention of the body, which is both the subject and the object, which represents and exposes itself. The moving body lives through the pulsation and circulation of its energies, establishes autonomous energy language, the characteristics of which are incessant reversals, velocity, discontinuity, dissemination, etc. The new kinetics can thus, according to Bernard, be understood as "the art of loss" (*l'art de la d(pense*): the art of loss in the sphere of the spectator's comprehension, for this following of the shadows of loss becomes the essential principle of the spectator's seeing, i.e. interpretation (embodied in contemporary performance art), but also the art of loss of the body itself. This is no longer the mimetic body, but the body that

4 Michel Bernard: "Les nouveaux codes corporeles de la danse contemporaine," in: *Le danse art du Xxe siecle?*, Editions Payot Lausanne, 1990, pp. 68-76.

★★★Autobiography self-promo booklet

A Day in May Design

CLIENT. Eve Billig
ART DIRECTOR/DESIGNER/ILLUSTRATOR. Eve Billig
TOOLS. QuarkXPress, Illustrator

PAPER. Classic Crest Duplex (cover); Synergy Line, Variety (chapters)
PRINTING. Full Circle Press

raphic designer's resume
VE BILLIG
1
BUILDING BLOCKS
2
PROCESS
3
ORK
EPILOGUE
eve billig
2900 pierce st. #2
san francisco, ca 94123
evebillig@hotmail.com
p: 415.567.7905

★★★"Peace Out" holiday greeting

Public

CLIENT. Public
ART DIRECTOR. Todd Foreman
DESIGNER. Tessa Lee

TOOLS. Illustrator, Macintosh
PAPER. French Frostone
PRINTING. San Francisco Center for the Book (by Public)

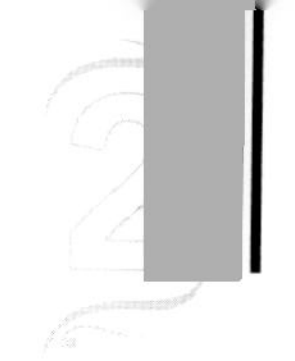

★★★Industry Films holiday card

Bløk Design

IT'S ABOUT A CURE. ON YOUR BEHALF WE MADE A DONATION TO THE AIDS COMMITTEE OF TORONTO AND TO THE BREAST CANCER SOCIETY OF CANADA. HAPPY HOLIDAYS + OUR BEST WISHES FOR 2001. FROM ALL OF US AT INDUSTRY FILMS

CLIENT. Industry Films
ART DIRECTOR. Vanessa Eckstein
DESIGNER. Stephanie Yung

TOOLS. Illustrator, Macintosh
PAPER. Strathmore
PRINTING. C.J. Graphics

★★★The Partners Formula Book

Bløk Design

CLIENT. The Partners Film Company
ART DIRECTOR. Vanessa Eckstein
DESIGNERS. Vanessa Eckstein, Frances Chen
TOOLS. Illustrator, Macintosh
PRINTING. C.J. Graphics

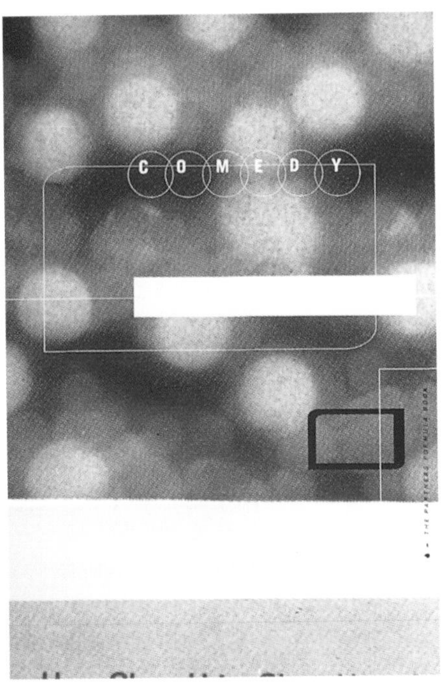

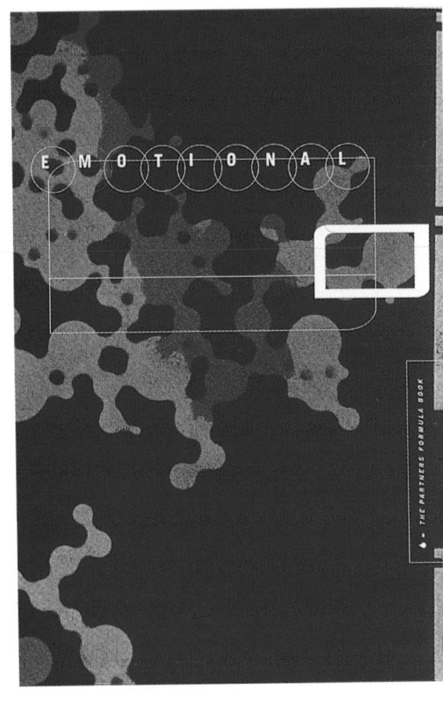

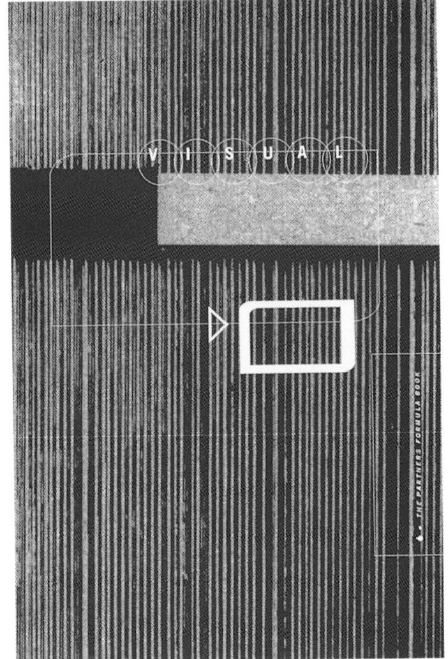

PARTNERS' TABLE OF ELEMENTS
15
Da Fa Ga Mc Dc Gd' Ch Bh Lm Bm Gs Fs
Ks Cs Ey Ma Mb Bh Il
Ap Gr Cs
6 Dm Ma Js Lds La Tr US
US Ta Nb Ab Sb Mb
Cb Sb Ad Jd Ne
Tf Df Jf Kf Tg
Jg Pj Jb Aj J
Nj Jk Kk Rlz Wm
Pm Bm Hpj Hp Np
Npk Mr Nr Lr Br
As Ss Cs Mt Kt
Jt Ov Wv Rw Mw
By 10 Mc Cc Sg Dg
Gh Gj Pm Gr Es Gw
tel: 416 869 3500

St C Vs F/B E
fernando arrioja
BILINGUAL: SPANISH
director
St D Rp Cs Em Vs
michael cerny
director

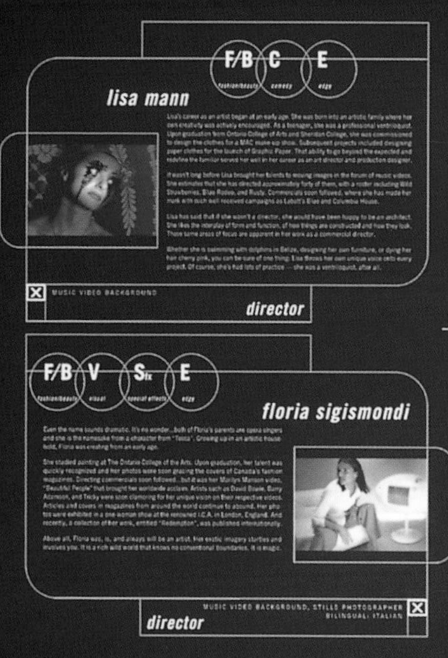

F/B C E
lisa mann
MUSIC VIDEO BACKGROUND
director
F/B V Sfx E
floria sigismondi
MUSIC VIDEO BACKGROUND, STILLS PHOTOGRAPHER
BILINGUAL: ITALIAN
director

★★★Gillespie Design holiday card

Gillespie Design, Inc.

CLIENT. Gillespie Design
ART DIRECTOR. Maureen Gillespie
DESIGNER. Liz Schenker
PRINTING. Offset, Lightning Copy

Biennale internationale de design graphique du Québec • deuxième édition
Quebec's International Graphic Design **Biennial** • second edition
Internationale graphische **vormgevingsbiennale** Québec • tweede aflevering

INVLOEDS
DENIS DULUDE 19.10.00 9 H AM
ZONE 18·22
octobre / october / oktober
2000 Montréal Canada
Pays-Bas Netherlands Nederland

'HOLLANDAIS, E adj. et n. De Hollande
◇ *Sauce hollandaise*, à base de jaunes d'œufs et de beurre, additionnée de jus de citron.

SOURCE : LE PETIT LAROUSSE ILLUSTRÉ 1997

MERCI À CAROLE ET BERNARD DE M'AVOIR SI GENTIMENT INVITÉ À CETTE DEUXIÈME ÉDITION DE LA BIENNALE. J'EN SUIS TRÈS HONORÉ.
MERCI À PHILIPPE ET MICHEL DE COMPLÈTEMENT LITHO POUR L'IMPRESSION DE CETTE AFFICHE.

CLIENT. KO Création
ART DIRECTOR/DESIGNER. Denis Dulude
TOOLS. Illustrator, Photostop, Macintosh
PRINTING. Sheet-fed offset

★★★Mo'nia stamps

Mo'nia

CLIENT. Mo'nia
ART DIRECTOR/DESIGNER/ ILLUSTRATOR. Mo'nia
TOOLS. Photoshop, Freehand, Macintosh

BY AIR MAIL
par avion
Royal Mail
51$
ptt post
P4579-1 (0293)-54037

RUIVO (LISBOA)
TAXA PAGA
51$

Gates
51$

51$

***Anni Kuan Design self-promotion

Sagmeister, Inc.

CLIENT. Anni Kuan Design
ART DIRECTOR. Stefan Sagmeister
DESIGNER/ILLUSTRATOR. Ella Smolarz

TOOLS. Illustrator, Photoshop
PAPER. Newsprint
PRINTING. Newsprint

A LINE SKIRT IN COCOA SILK TWEED W/ ULTRA SUEDE TRIM

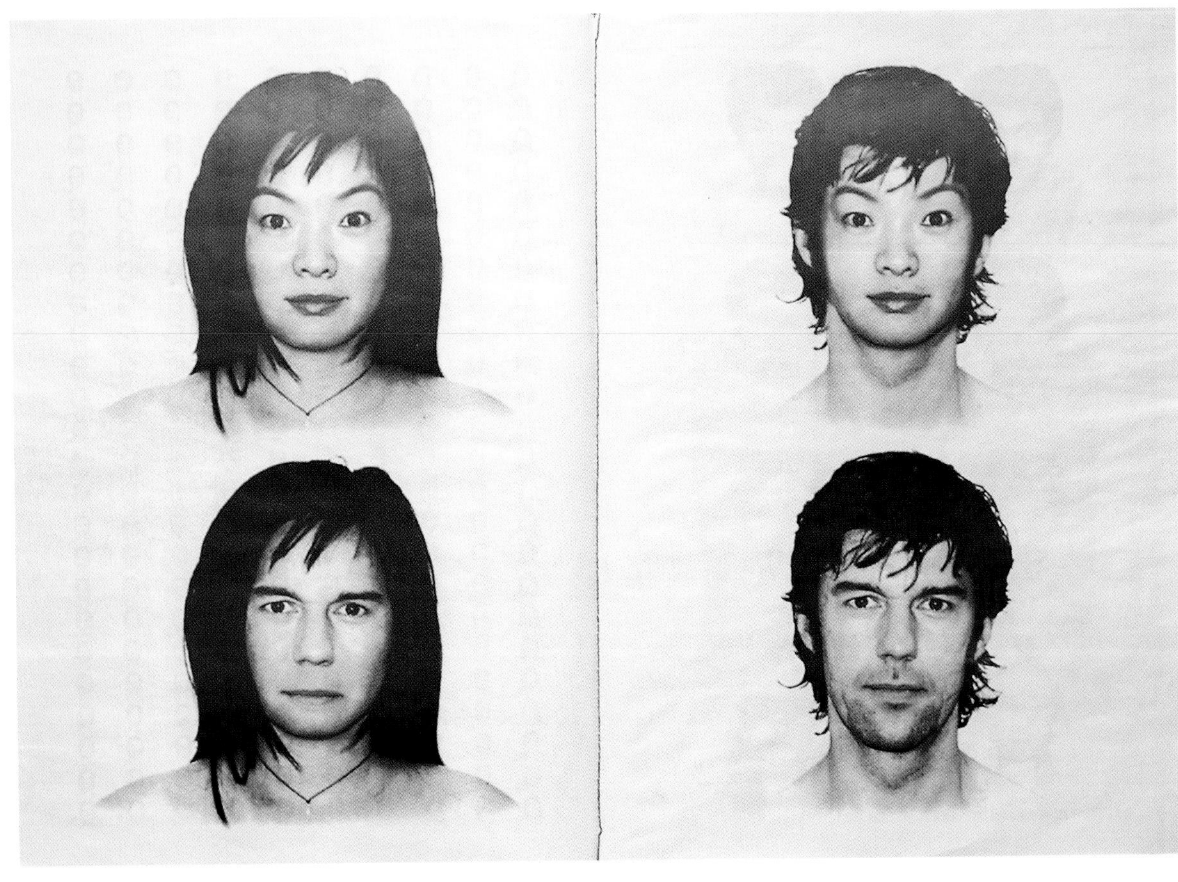

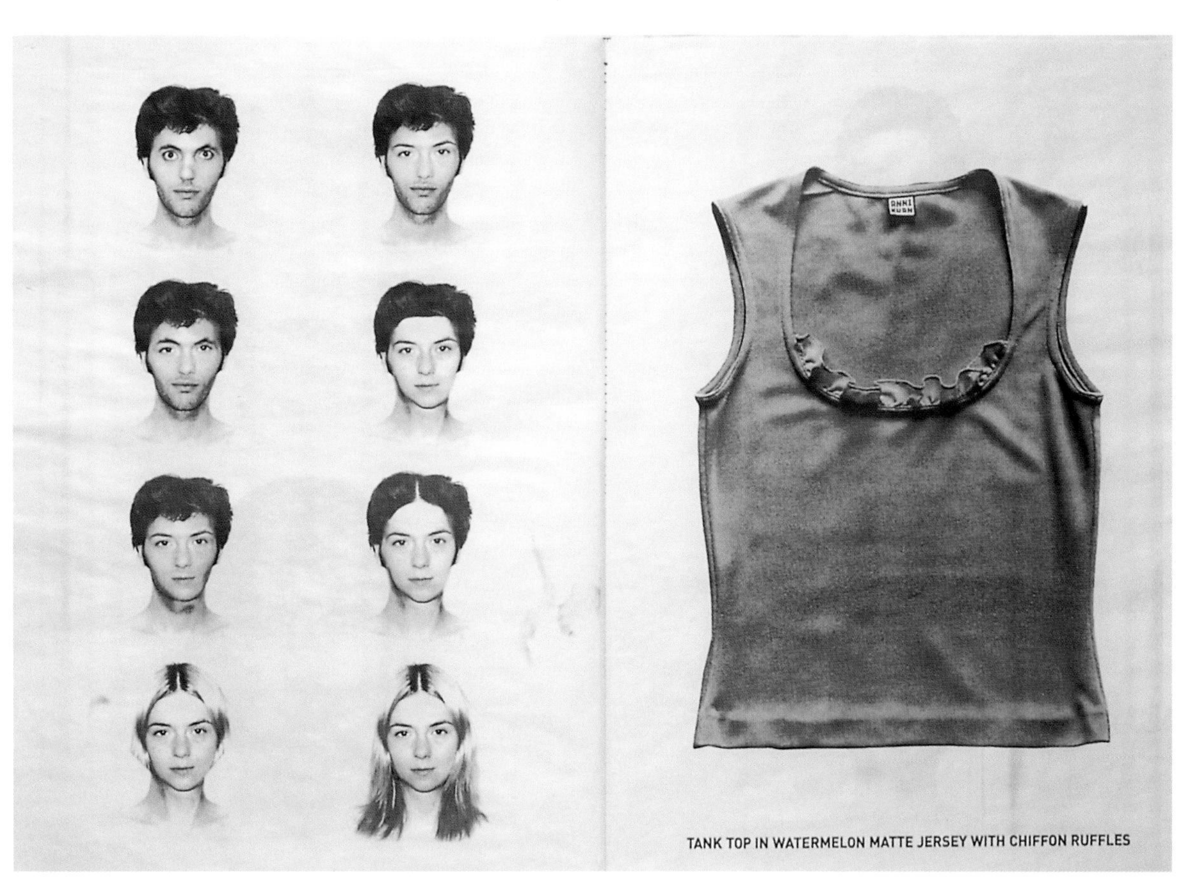

TANK TOP IN WATERMELON MATTE JERSEY WITH CHIFFON RUFFLES

★★★Anni Kuan Design self-promotion

Sagmeister, Inc.

CLIENT. Anni Kuan Design
ART DIRECTOR. Stefan Sagmeister
DESIGNERS. Stefan Sagmeister, Hjalti Karlsson

TOOLS. Illustrator, Photoshop
PAPER. Newsprint
PRINTING. Newsprint

PHOTOGRAPH OF
NEW YORK CITY
SKYLINE REFLECTED
IN RAIN PUDDLE.

PHOTOGRAPH OF
ANNI KUAN
EMBROIDERED LABEL,
THREADS SHOWING.

SUPER SHARP PHOTOGRAPH OF LUMPS OF BLACK COAL, ARRANGED TO TAKE THE SAME OUTLINE SHAPE AS DARK HAIRED MODEL ON OPPOSITE PAGE.

PHOTOGRAPH OF DARK HAIRED MODEL (WITH LIGHT MUSTACHE) IN ANNI KUAN BLACK RAYON MATTE JERSEY FLOOR-LENGTH DRESS WITH A LOW V-NECK FRONT AND BELL SLEEVES WITH BLACK FUR TRIM.

PHOTOGRAPH OF RED STRING, LYING LOOSELY AND RESEMBLING BORED BLOND WOMAN.

PHOTOGRAPH OF BORED BLOND WOMAN, ONE BREAST SHOWING, CARRYING NAKED BABY, IN A LIPSTICK RED FUZZY ANGORA LOW-CUT BALLERINA TOP OVER A MULTI-COLORED COLLAGED SILK CHARMEUSE BIAS-CUT LONG SKIRT.

PHOTO OF RECLINING RED HAIRED GIRL WEARING LARGE SQUARE SUNGLASSES AND LICKING CHERRY LOLLIPOP IN BLOOD ORANGE DOUBLEKNIT TEE WITH MOHAIR CORD TRIM WORN OVER BROWN STRETCH WOOL CROPPED PANTS WITH SHAGGY CHENILLE CUFFS, ACCESSORIZED WITH A BERRY MOHAIR TOTE BAG.

PHOTOGRAPHIC IMAGE OF 3 BRICKS GROUPED TO RESEMBLE CONTOUR OF RED HAIRED GIRL.

SCION

★★★Al Fitr holiday greeting

Nassar Design

CLIENT. Harvard School of Government
ART DIRECTOR/DESIGNER. Nelida Nassar

TOOLS. QuarkXPress, Photoshop
PAPER. Champion Benefit 100#C
PRINTING. Offset

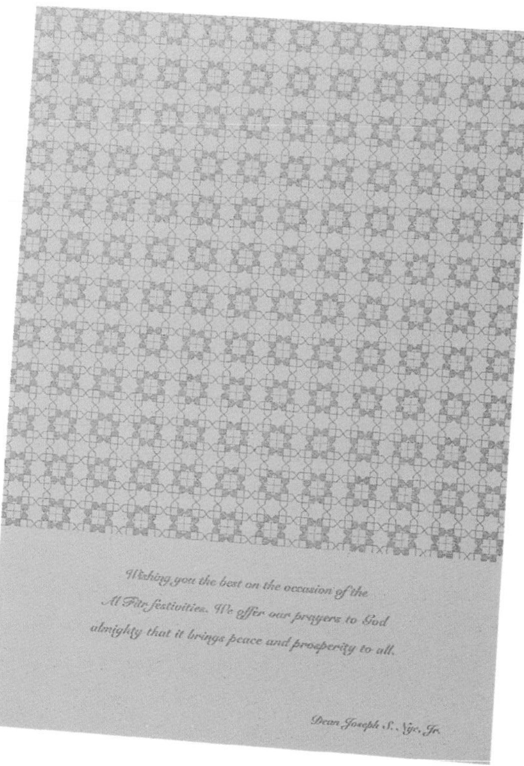

CLIENT. Seth Affoumado
ART DIRECTOR/DESIGNER. Tom Sieu

TOOLS. Photoshop, QuarkXPress, Macintosh, photocopy
PAPER. Black Uncoated Recycled Stock
PRINTING. Offset

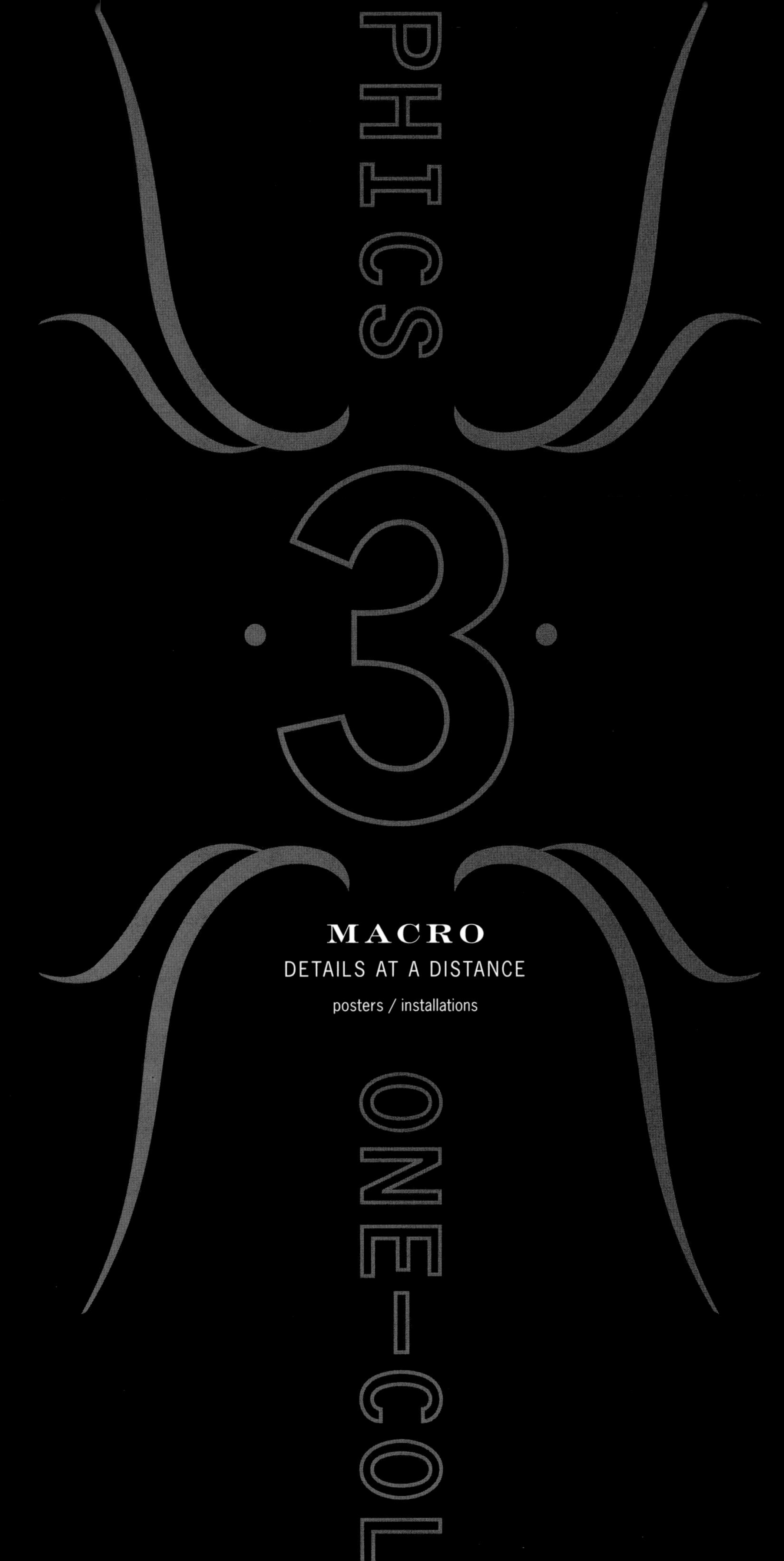

3

MACRO

DETAILS AT A DISTANCE

posters / installations

★★CCAC posters

Morla Design

CLIENT. California College of Arts & Crafts
ART DIRECTOR. Jennifer Morla
DESIGNERS. Sara Schneider, Jennifer Morla
TOOLS. QuarkXPress, Illustrator, Photoshop, Macintosh
PAPER. Newsprint
PRINTING. Offset, black ink

the ccacInstitute presents
fabrice hybert:
at your own risk
the logan galleries, ccac, 1111 8th street [16th street at wisconsin] san francisco
april 17–june 5, 1999
gallery hours: 11am–5pm monday, wednesday, thursday, friday, and saturday.
11am–9pm tuesday. admission is free. the facility is wheelchair accessible.
information: 415.551.9210.

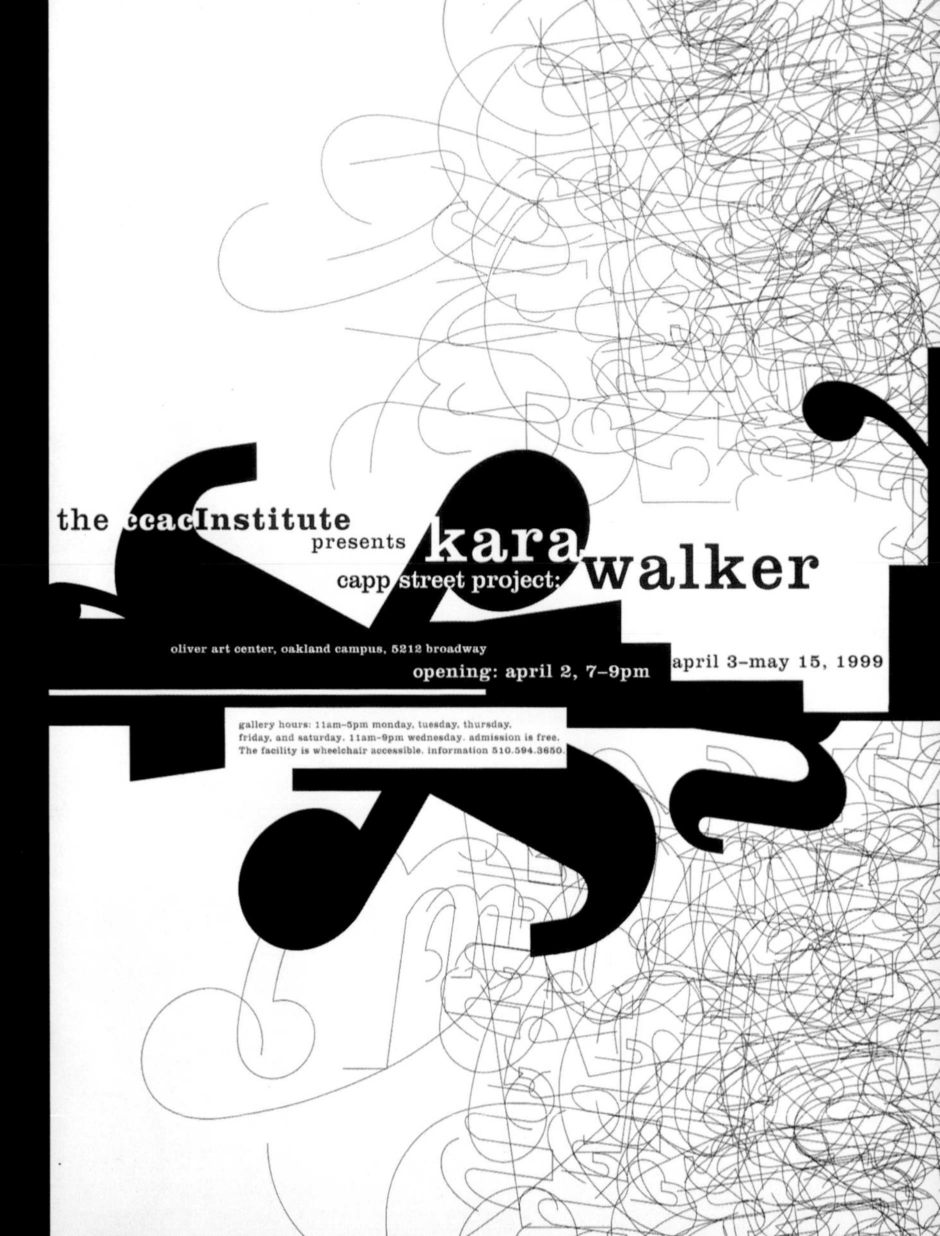
the ccacInstitute
presents
kara
capp street project:
walker
oliver art center, oakland campus, 5212 broadway
opening: april 2, 7–9pm
april 3–may 15, 1999
gallery hours: 11am–5pm monday, tuesday, thursday, friday, and saturday. 11am–9pm wednesday. admission is free. The facility is wheelchair accessible. information 510.594.3650.

the ccacInstitute
presents

spaced out:

late 1990s works from the collection of vicki and kent logan

the logan galleries, ccac, 1111 8th street [16th street at wisconsin] san francisco

april 17–june 5, 1999

gallery hours: 11am–5pm monday, wednesday, thursday, friday, and saturday.
11am–9pm tuesday. admission is free. the facility is wheelchair accessible.
information: 415.551.9210.

★★★Exhibition poster

Friedhelm Plassmeier

CLIENT. Society for Christian and Jewish Partnership
DESIGNER. Friedhelm Plassmeier

A U S S T E L L U N G

FOTOS AUS DEM WARSCHAUER GHETTO

Die Fotos werden von der Gesellschaft für Christlich-Jüdische Zusammenarbeit Paderborn e.V. zur Verfügung gestellt.

6.11.–27.11.01

Gymnasium St. Xaver
IN DER AULA

Öffnungszeiten: Während der Unterrichtszeit und nach Vereinbarung unter Bad Driburg Tel.: 0 52 53 / 40 22 53

Tom & John: A Design Collaborative

★★★Prairie Sun poster

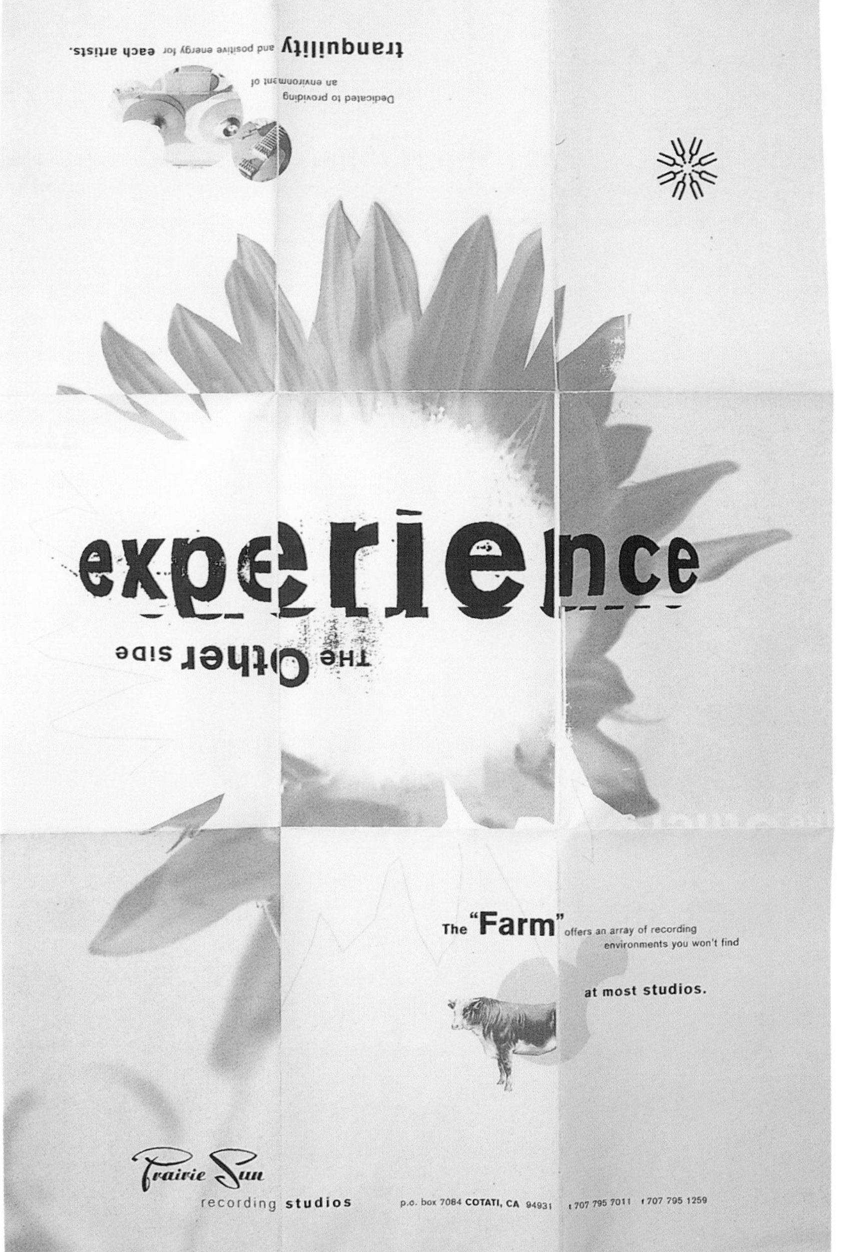

CLIENT. Prairie Sun Recording Studios
ART DIRECTOR/DESIGNER. Tom Sieu
TOOLS. Photoshop, QuarkXPress, Macintosh
PAPER. Uncoated Industrial Recycled
PRINTING. Diazo

★★★Love Square & Circle

Studio International

CLIENT. Museum Documentation Croatia
ART DIRECTOR/DESIGNER/ILLUSTRATOR. Boris Ljubičić

TOOLS. Corel, PC
PAPER. Kunstdruck 250g
PRINTING. Silkscreen

International
Museum
Day
Love
18.0
COM

★★★"Art" poster
Lure Design, Inc.

CLIENT. Orlando–UCF Shakespeare Festival
DESIGNERS. Paul Mastriani, Jeff Matz
TOOLS. Illustrator, Photoshop
PAPER. Mohawk textures, Ultrafelt
PRINTING. Offset with embossing

TICKETS FOR JEWEL AVAILABLE AT SAPPHIRE, TICKET MASTER, WAXTREE RECORDS, MURMUR RECORDS, PARK AVENUE CD, RECORD VAULT, EAST-WEST RECORDS, SONIC BOOM
7 O'CLOCK
jewel
with duncan shiek
TEN DOLLARS (AND STAY FOR THE GRIFTERS)
SAPPHIRE SUPPER CLUB
★ MEMORIAL DAY ★
MAY 27TH 1996
ELEVEN O'CLOCK LATE SHOW
Grifters
+ BRAILLE CLOSET USA
5 Dollars

★★★"Woman in Black" posters

Lure Design, Inc.

CLIENT. Orlando–UCF Shakespeare Festival
DESIGNERS. Paul Mastriani, Jeff Matz
TOOLS. Illustrator, Photoshop

PAPER. Fraser Pegasus Midnight Black Vellum
PRINTING. Offset, silver ink

a ghost story

Adapted by Stephen Mallatratt
From the book by Susan Hill

ORLANDO-UCF SHAKESPEARE FESTIVAL

September 22 through October 29, 2000

The Goldman Theater, Shakespeare Theater Center, Loch Haven Park

Tickets $16 & $20 Box Office {407} 893-4600

Sponsored by WMFE TV/FM

★★★"Woman in Black" posters—continued

★★★ "How Do You Know What You Know?" posters
Cabra Diseño

CLIENT. San Francisco AIDS Foundation
ART DIRECTOR. Raul Cabra
DESIGNERS. Mark Santa Ana, Wesley Ito, Betty Ho
PHOTOGRAPHER. Ken Probst
TOOLS. QuarkXPress, Macintosh
PAPER. Cougar Untreated 86#C
PRINTING. Gateway Graphics

I DON'T
HAVE IT YET.
I MUST BE
IMMUNE.

HOW DO YOU KNOW
WHAT YOU KNOW?

www.gaylife.org
415.863.AIDS

EVENTS, WORKSHOPS, COUNSELING

FUNDED IN PART BY THE CALIFORNIA WELLNESS FOUNDATION. PHOTOGRAPHY: KEN PROBST ©2001. DESIGN: CABRA DISEÑO: RAUL CABRA, MARK SANTA ANA, WESLEY ITO, BETTY HO. TEXT: JON ROEMER

HE'D TELL ME IF HE'S POSITIVE.

HE'D TELL ME IF HE'S NEGATIVE.

HOW DO YOU KNOW WHAT YOU KNOW?

www.gaylife.org
415.863.AIDS

GAY LIFE

EVENTS, WORKSHOPS, COUNSELING

FUNDED IN PART BY THE CALIFORNIA WELLNESS FOUNDATION. PHOTOGRAPHY: KEN PROBST ©2001. DESIGN: CABRA DISEÑO: RAUL CABRA, MARK SANTA ANA, WESLEY ITO, BETTY HO. TEXT: JON ROEMER

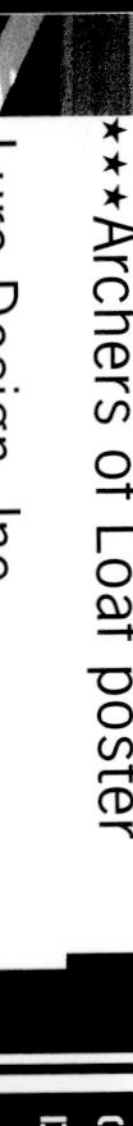

★★★Archers of Loaf poster
Lure Design, Inc.

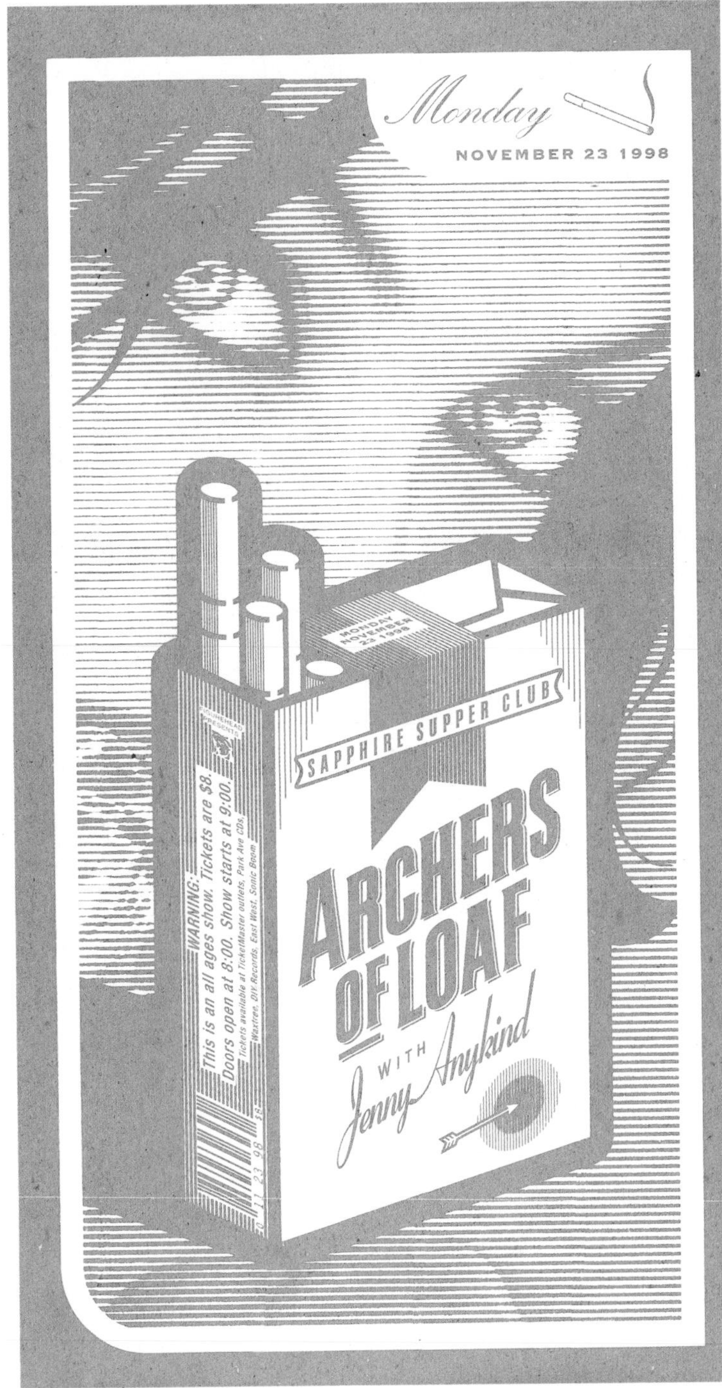

CLIENT. Figurehead Records
DESIGNER/ILLUSTRATOR. Jeff Matz

TOOLS. Illustrator, Photoshop
PAPER. Chipboard
PRINTING. Silkscreen

FIGUREHEAD AND PARK AVE CDS PRESENT
SAPPHIRE SUPPER CLUB
Elliott Smith
with no.2
TEN DOLLARS GENERAL ADMISSION
DOORS OPEN AT 8:00 SHOW AT 9:00
THIS IS AN ALL AGES SHOW
TICKETS AT ALL TICKETMASTER LOCATIONS
PARK AVE CDS, WAX TREE, SONIC BOOM
AND EAST WEST RECORDS
MONDAY
March 15

★★★Multimedia Institute MIZ
Arkzin d.o.o.

CLIENT. Multimedia Institute Miz, Zagreb, Croatia
ART DIRECTOR. Dejan Dragosavac-Rutta
DESIGNERS. Dejan Dragosavac, Dejan Kršić
TOOLS. Freehand, Photoshop
PRINTING. Offset

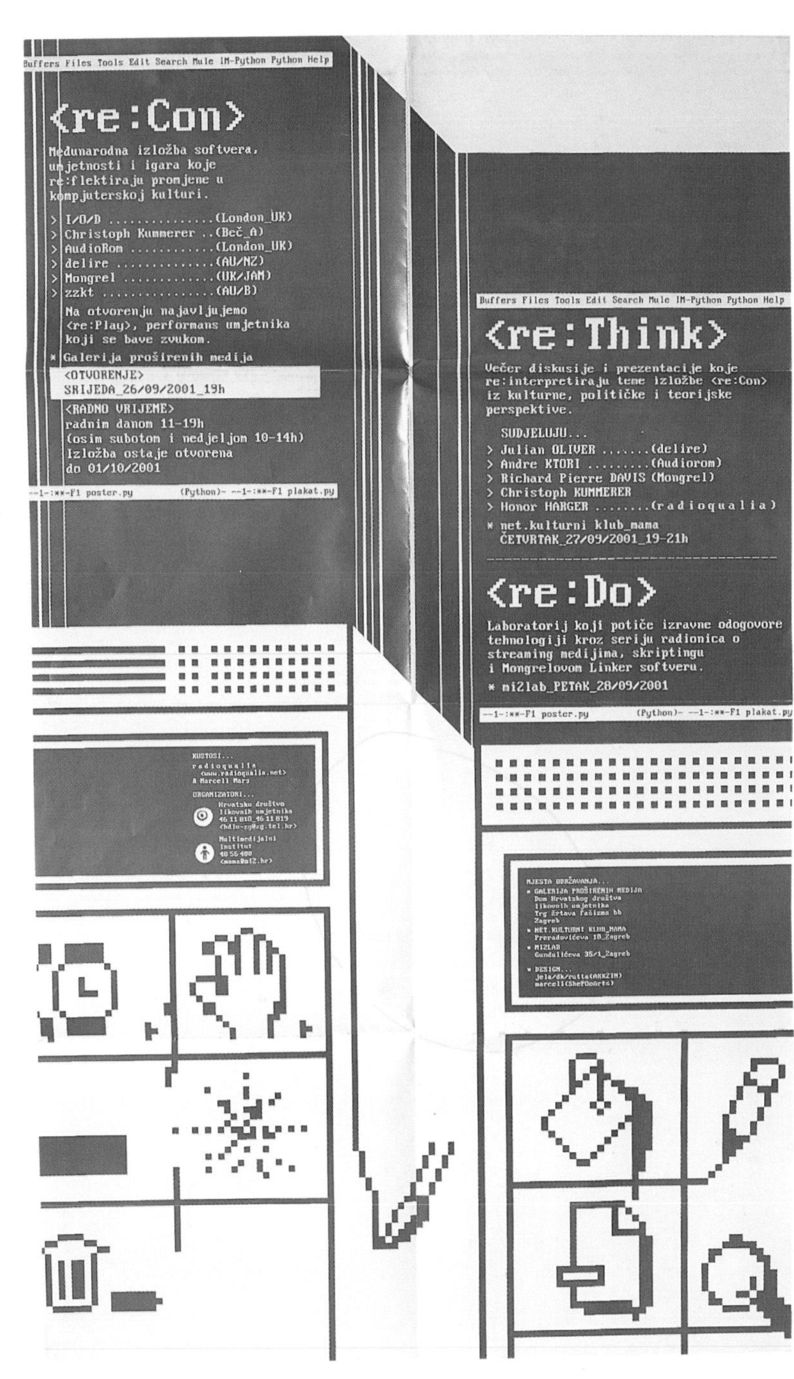

1C/C

MACRO

★★★2000 MFA Exhibit poster

University of Washington

2000

HENRY ART GALLERY

THE HENRY is located at 15th Avenue NE and NE 41st Street. Tuesday, Wednesday, Friday, Saturday, Sunday from 11-5 and Thursday 11-8. 206-543-2280 www.henryart.org for more information.

F

(master of the fine arts)

. M A

: EXHIBIT

university of washington
school of art

reception Friday May 26 5:00-8:00pm

MAY 27 - JUNE 25

TOOLS. Illustrator, Macintosh
PAPER. Lustro Archival Dull 100 #T
PRINTING. Olympus Press

CLIENT. University of Washington School of Art
DESIGNER. Karen Cheng

Fest
100 Jahre
Rathausbühne
Willisau
14./15.sept.
'01

★★★Jazz in Willisau poster
Niklaus Troxler Design

CLIENT. Jazz in Willisau
ART DIRECTOR/DESIGNER. Niklaus Troxler
PAPER. Poster, 90.5 x 128 cm
PRINTING. Silkscreen

★★★Jazz in Willisau poster
Niklaus Troxler Design

CLIENT. Jazz in Willisau
ART DIRECTOR/DESIGNER. Niklaus Troxler
PAPER. Poster, 90.5 x 128 cm
PRINTING. Silkscreen

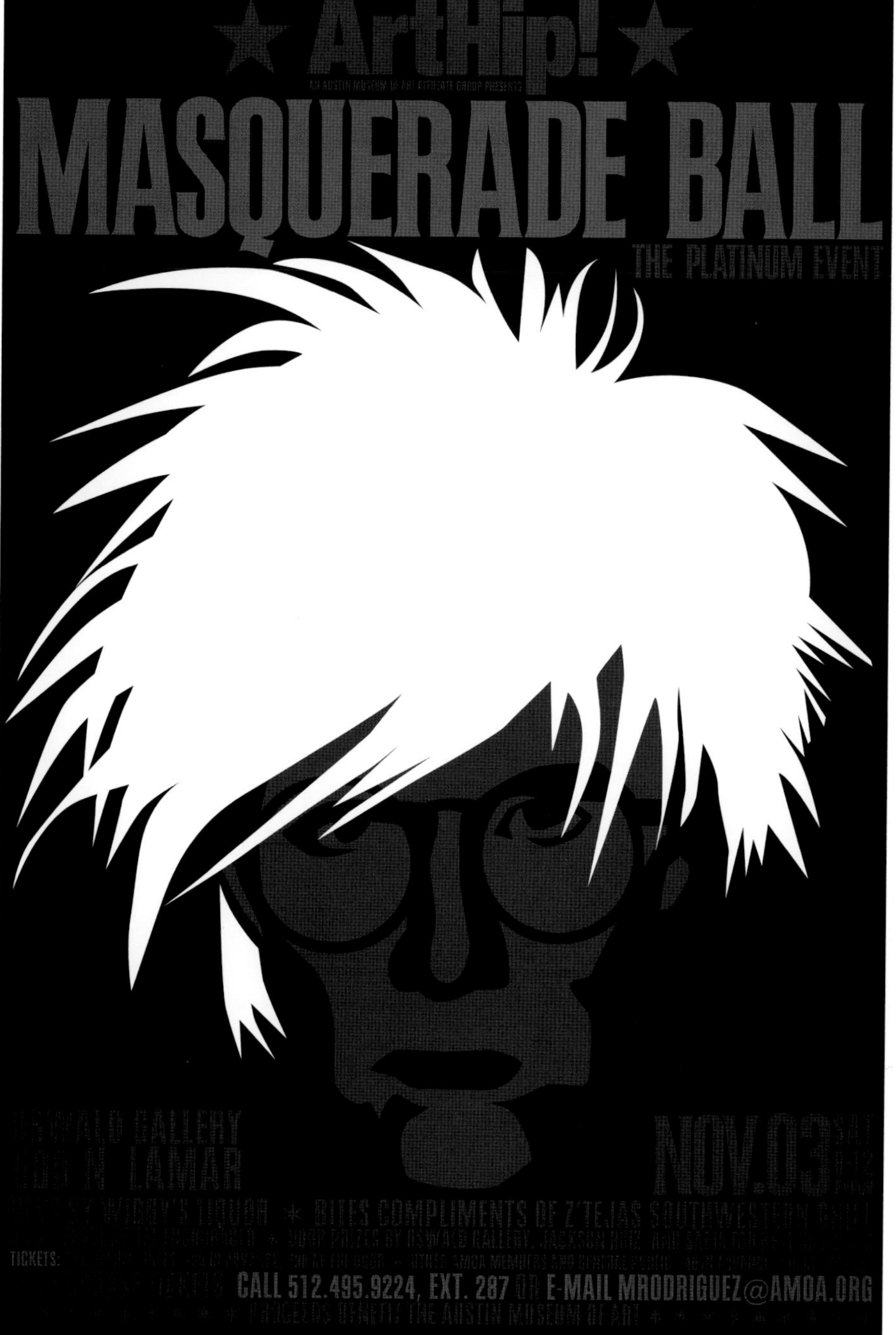

★★★ArtHip! Masquerade Ball poster

Shoehorn Design

CLIENT. Austin Museum of Art
ART DIRECTOR. Will Hornaday
DESIGNERS. Ted Roddy, Will Hornaday
ILLUSTRATOR. Will Hornaday
TOOLS. Illustrator, Macintosh
PAPER. Quantum Opaque White 80#C
PRINTING. The Whitley Company

★★★October 18 lecture poster

Jennifer Sterling Design

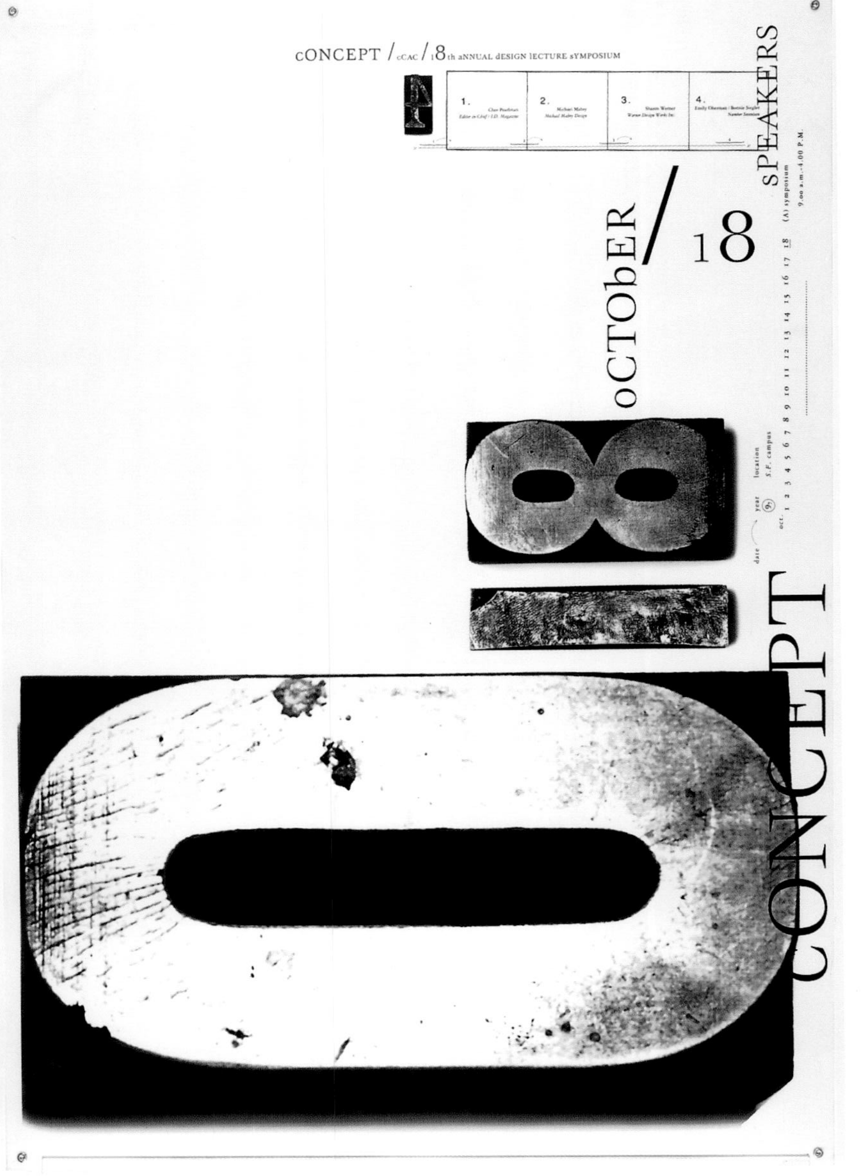

CLIENT. California College of Arts and Crafts
ART DIRECTOR/DESIGNER. Jennifer Sterling
TOOLS. Illustrator, Photoshop, Macintosh

MATERIALS. Lexan
PRINTER. Bel Aire Display

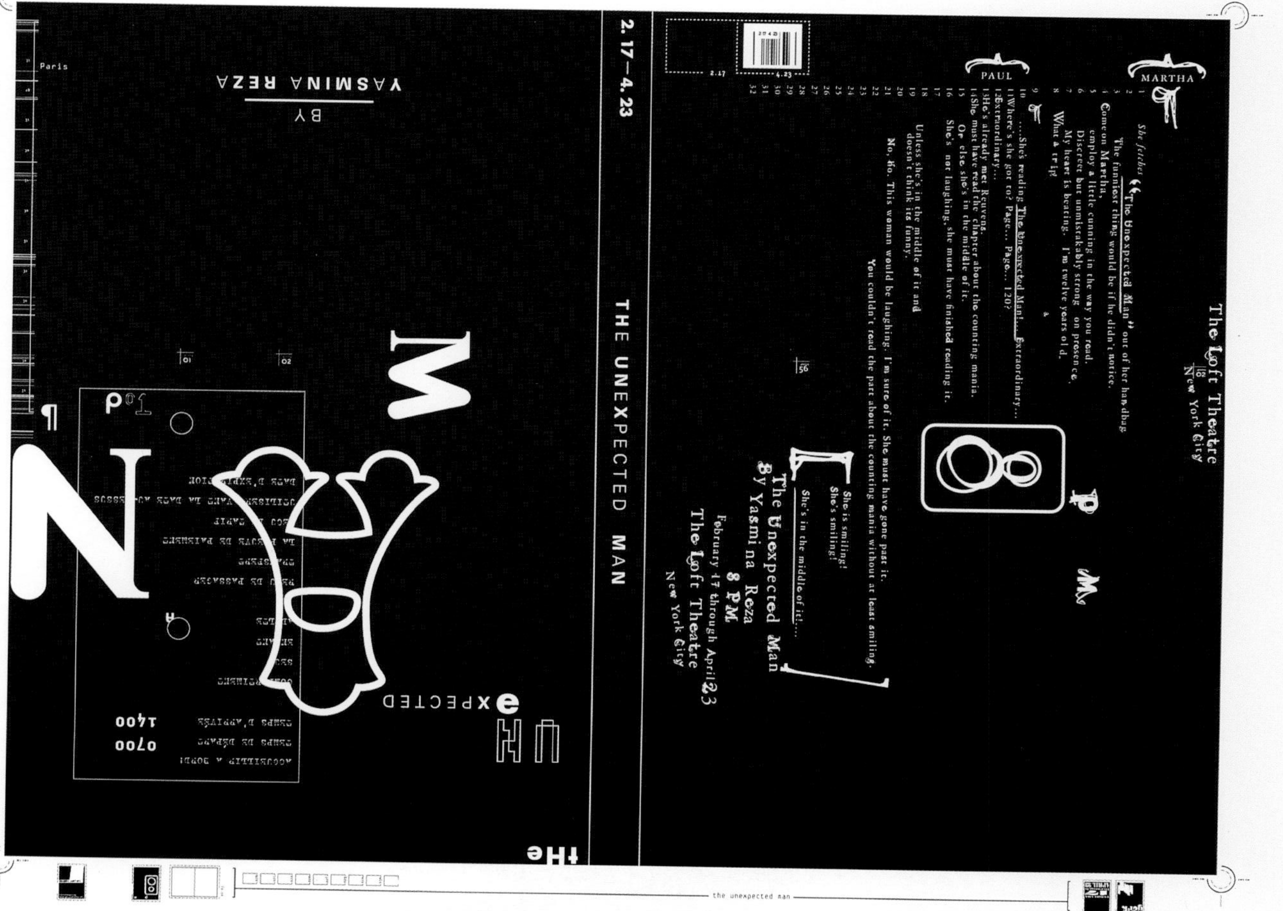

CLIENT. *Critique* magazine
ART DIRECTOR/DESIGNER. Jennifer Sterling

TOOLS. Illustrator, Macintosh
PAPER. Arches Watercolor
PRINTING. Trillium

★★★Unexpected Man poster

Jennifer Sterling Design

THE PATTERN
HEART OF SNOW
LOST KIDS
FRIDAY FEB. 23
THE PORTLITE
229 BRUSH ST.
OAKLAND
21+ $5

★★★Café du Nord poster

Red Alert Visuals

CLIENT. Café du Nord
ART DIRECTOR/DESIGNER. Jason Rosenberg
TOOLS. QuarkXPress, Photoshop, Streamline
PAPER. 60# Coated
PRINTING. Hand-screened

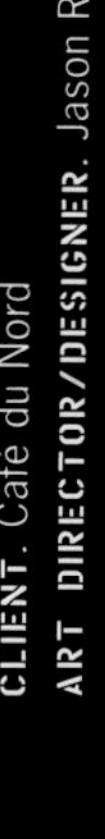

★★★Unplug KBOO 90.7 FM
Cheevers

CLIENT. Advocates for KBOO Community Radio
ART DIRECTOR/DESIGNER/ILLUSTRATOR. Tom Cheevers
TOOLS. QuarkXPress, Photoshop, Macintosh, photocopy
PAPER. French Dur-O-Tone Aged Newsprint
PRINTING. Kinkos

LISTENING TO THE RADIO MAY BE
TURNING
YOU
INTO A
HOMOSEXUAL.

With programs like "THIS WAY OUT" *and* "QUEER, QUEER WORLD," *it's obvious what flag of pride* KBOO [90.7 FM] *is waving — and it's not the Stars and Stripes. Your teenager may be* LISTENING *to rock & roll one minute and the next is being* HYPNOTIZED *by subliminal homosexual recruitment messages. They call themselves* GAY *but there's nothing happy about seeing a child sucked down the slippery slope of moral decay. The Sodomites at* KBOO [90.7 FM] *have* VIOLATED *our ears long enough. Straighten out, America! Resist* KBOO [90.7 FM] *and resist the* DEVIL'S DESIRES.

CONVINCED? VOTE BELOW!

YES! *Unplug KBOO before it's TOO LATE!*

SEND $5 FOR YOUR BUMPER STICKER.
Name: ______
Address: ______ *City:* ______ *State:* ______ *Zip:* ______
Send To: UNPLUG KBOO, 408 *SW 2nd Ave. Suite 411, Portland, Oregon 97204*

NO! *Don't unplug KBOO. I like it PLUGGED IN.*

★ ★ ★ PAID FOR BY THE COALITION OF INTOLERANT AMERICANS ★ ★ ★

e-mail: UNPLUGKBOO@AOL.COM

TRIP-HOP
SALSA
FUNK:
YOUR RADIO
CAN GET YOUR DAUGHTER
PREGNANT.

It starts innocently enough. A group of young people gather at the home of an ABSENT *parent. Then someone tunes the radio to* KBOO [90.7 FM]. *As darkness falls, the room fills with the* PULSING *rhythms of the station's sexually suggestive melodies. Soon all are rhythmically gyrating to the the lewd beat of* SATAN'S *hellish heart. For some unlucky woman this living nightmare may end nine months later with an unexpected dance partner. For* LIFE. *If this picture of moral* CORRUPTION *scares you, turn on traditional family values by turning off the most* DESTRUCTIVE *force in America today:* KBOO [90.7 FM] *radio.*

CONVINCED? VOTE BELOW!

YES! *Unplug KBOO before it's TOO LATE!*

SEND $5 FOR YOUR BUMPER STICKER.
Name: ______
Address: ______ *City:* ______ *State:* ______ *Zip:* ______
Send To: UNPLUG KBOO, 408 *SW 2nd Ave. Suite 411, Portland, Oregon 97204*

NO! *Don't unplug KBOO. I'm trying to GET PREGNANT!*

★ ★ ★ PAID FOR BY THE COALITION OF INTOLERANT AMERICANS ★ ★ ★

e-mail: UNPLUGKBOO@AOL.COM

WHEN KBOO RADIO SHOVES THE GRATEFUL DEAD DOWN YOUR THROAT, THE EVIL WEED IS SURE TO FOLLOW.

At KBOO [90.7 FM] *the psychopharmacological hell-hole that was the 60s never ended. It lives on in the form of* "THE GRATEFUL DEAD HOUR," *a mind-numbing collection of* "BOOGIE JAMS." *If the entire nation followed the pied-piper call of these hacky-sack hooligans, where would we be? Stuck on a collective farm answering* "YES, COMRADE" *to our Communist enslavers. It's time for these* FREE-LOVE *freaks to put down their pipes, shave their* DREADLOCKS, *enlist in the Army and become God-fearing Americans. Unplug* KBOO [90.7 FM] *before the stench of pot smoke makes us all coke-headed* ZOMBIES.

CONVINCED? VOTE BELOW!

YES!
Unplug KBOO before it's TOO LATE!

SEND $5 FOR YOUR BUMPER STICKER.

Name: ______________________

Address: ____________ *City:* ______ *State:* ____ *Zip:* ______

Send To: UNPLUG KBOO, 408 *SW 2nd Ave. Suite* 411, *Portland, Oregon* 97204

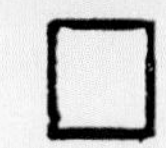

NO!
Don't unplug KBOO. Jerry's not dead, he just SMELLS FUNNY.

★ ★ ★ **PAID FOR BY THE COALITION OF INTOLERANT AMERICANS** ★ ★ ★

e-mail: UNPLUGKBOO@AOL.COM

★★★"No Matter" poster
MATTER

CLIENT. MATTER
ART DIRECTOR. Jason C. Otero

DESIGNERS. Jason C. Otero, Rick Griffith, Joe Lamarre, Shennon Murray, Paco Proano

TOOLS. Imagination, Bare Hands
PAPER. Various
PRINTING. Screenprinting

NO HURTING
FXIT
NO KING
BEWARE of GOD
PEEK OUT!
Come in CLOSE
Sorry WE'RE OPEN
NO MATTER

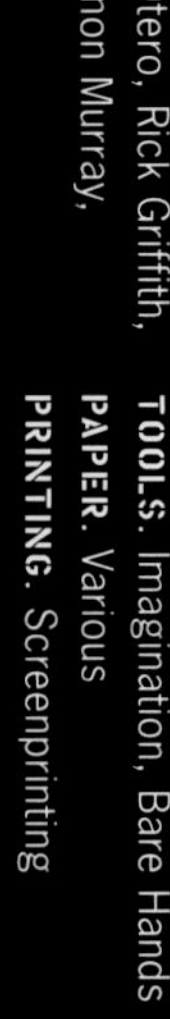

JULY
CREATIVE MUSIC SERIES
JULY 5 HAPPY LIZARD
rick Cummings -guitar
ernie Crews - drums
john Britten - electric bass
JULY 12 MU TOO TA TOR
[trumpet • electronics • sax • poetry]
tom Djll (from san-francisco)
w/ hillary Double d
JULY 19 THE INSTRUMENT PANEL
mike O'neil - guitar
farrell Lowe - guitar
gordon kennedy - drums
terry Sines - acoustic bass
JULY 26 ENSEMBLE
richard Turco - woodwinds/composition
w/jennifer Turco - woodwinds
& tim Lenk - keys
tuesdays
UNLESS OTHERWISE NOTED ALL PERFORMANCES ARE AT THE WEST END TAVERN 926 PEARL STREET (303) 444-3535
for more information call (303) 440-5638
design: rick griffith design, boulder

★★★An Audio Obstacle Course
MATTER

CLIENT. Creative Music Series
ART DIRECTOR/DESIGNER. Rick Griffith
TOOLS. QuarkXPress, Macintosh
PAPER/PRINTING. Blueline

★★★The Jazz Series: Craig Handy poster

CLIENT. Miller Theater
ART DIRECTOR/DESIGNER. Rick Griffith
TOOLS. QuarkXPress, Macintosh
PAPER/PRINTING. Brownline

★★★Innerschweizer Filmtage poster

Mix Pictures Grafik

CLIENT. Kleintheater Luzern
ART DIRECTOR/DESIGNER. Erich Brechbühl

TOOLS. Freehand, Macintosh
PAPER. Poster
PRINTING. Silkscreen

★★★ Jugendtheater Sempach poster
Mix Pictures Grafik

CLIENT. Jugendtheater Sempach
ART DIRECTOR/DESIGNER. Erich Brechbühl
TOOLS. Photoshop, Macintosh
PAPER. Poster
PRINTING. Silkscreen

4
MICRO
AN INTIMATE IMPRESSION
invitations / announcements

CLIENTS. Ellen Bruni-Gillies & Dan Gillies
ART DIRECTOR/DESIGNER. Ellen Bruni-Gillies
ILLUSTRATOR. Ward Shumacher

TOOLS. QuarkXPress, Photoshop, Macintosh
PAPER. Fox River Teton Tiara White
PRINTING. Full Circle Press

★★★Milo birth announcement

Ellen Bruni-Gillies Design

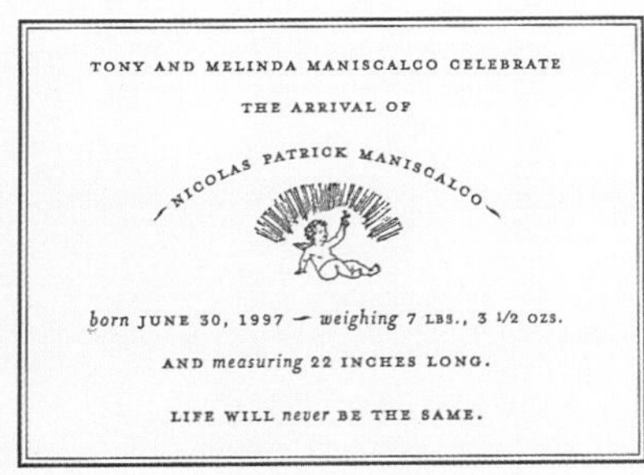

CLIENTS. Melinda and Tony Maniscalco
ART DIRECTORS/DESIGNERS. Melinda and Tony Maniscalco
ILLUSTRATOR. Clip art
TOOLS. Illustrator, Macintosh
PRINTING. Full Circle Press

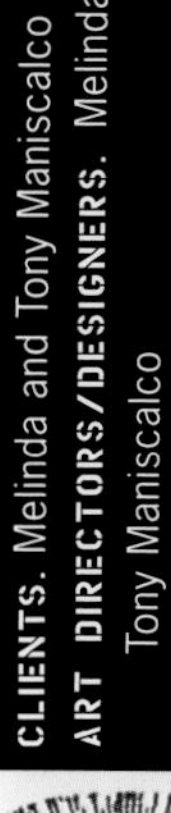

★★★Nicolas and Luca birth announcements

Homespun Design

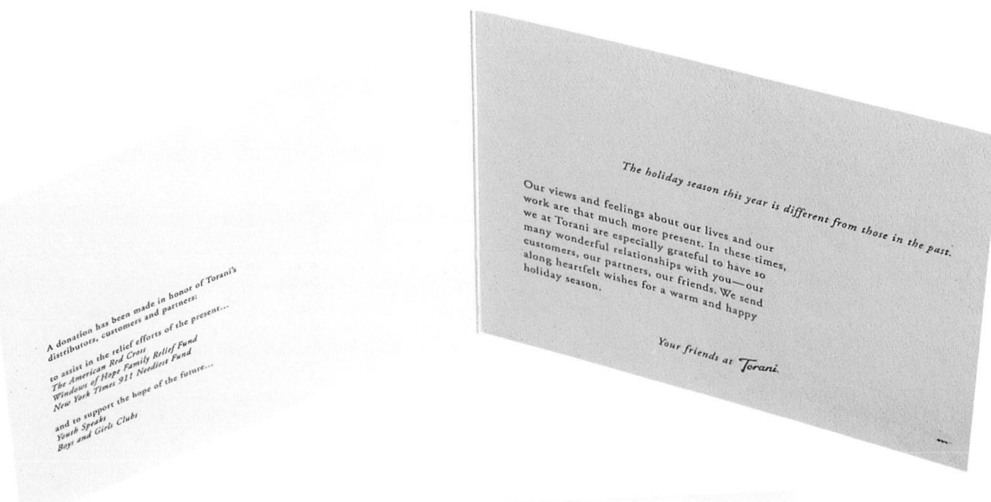

CLIENT. Torani
ART DIRECTOR/ILLUSTRATOR. Laura Bauer
DESIGNER. Gary Wong
TOOLS. Illustrator, Macintosh
PRINTING. Full Circle Press

★★★Torani holiday card

Anvil Graphic Design

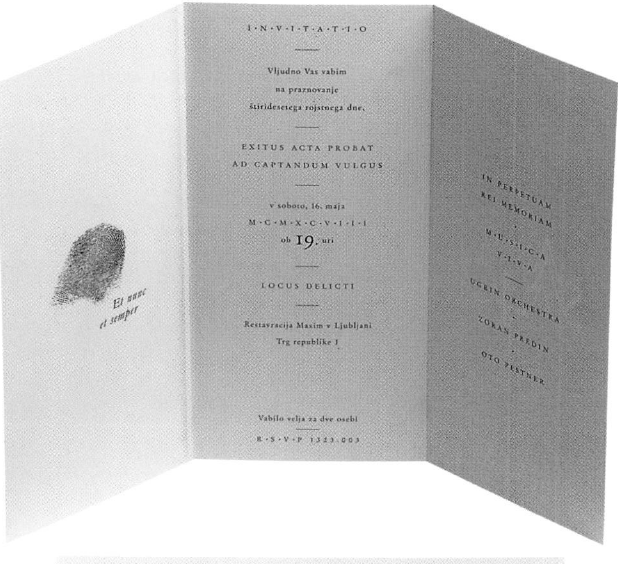

CLIENT. Miro Senica
ART DIRECTOR/DESIGNER. Edi Berk
TOOLS. Illustrator, Macintosh
PAPER. Conqueror Vergata
PRINTING. Offset

***Anno Aetatis Suae 40 invitation

KROG

The VENTURA COUNTY STAR and the
VENTURA COUNTY MEDICAL RESOURCE FOUNDATION
present the

NINTH ANNUAL
DAVID C. FAINER M.D.
AWARDS DINNER

PROGRAM RECORD

CLINIC OFFICE: SPANISH HILLS GOLF & COUNTRY CLUB

THIS RECORD MAY BE REMOVED FROM THE SITE

Feel free to remove this record from designated area without notifying Medical Records

INFORMATION IN THIS RECORD IS NOT CONFIDENTIAL

PATIENT'S NAME
LAST
FIRST
MIDDLE

2005	2004	2003	2002	2001	2000	1999	1998	1997	1996	1995	1994	1993
				■								

CLIENT. Ventura County Medical Resource Foundation
ART DIRECTOR. Barbara Brown
DESIGNER. Alicia Hoskins
TOOLS. QuarkXPress, Macintosh
PAPER. French

★★★Fainer Awards Dinner invite and program

Barbara Brown Marketing & Design

PLACE
STAMP

PRESCRIPTION

Name: NINTH ANNUAL DAVID C. FAINER M.D. AWARDS DINNER

Date: NOVEMBER 2, 2001

Place: SPANISH HILLS GOLF & COUNTRY CLUB

Attire: BLACK TIE OPTIONAL

Sig: Evening festivities
Silent Auction & No-Host Bar 6:15 pm
Dinner/Program 7:45 pm

Disp: One fun Evening!

Instructions: Register early for best bed assignment

John Keats, M.D.
Master of Ceremonies

Refill: Annually

VENTURA COUNTY
MEDICAL RESOURCE FOUNDATION
250 Citrus Grove Lane Suite 240
Oxnard, California 93030

ADDRESS SERVICE REQUESTED

I've schedu...
appoint...
DIAGNOSIS:

Ninth Annual David C. Fainer M.D. Awards Dinner

HISTORY and PHYSICAL

Please fill out and take a seat. The Doctor will be with you shortly.

Name:
Address:
City: State: Zip:
Telephone:

[] I/We want to be a Gold Sponsor for $2,500* with VIP seating for 12.
(Includes 1/4 page ad in program, recognition as Gold sponsor in publicity materials and at dinner.)
[] I/We want to be a Silver Sponsor for $1,000* with VIP seating for 4.
(Includes 1/8 page ad in program, recognition as Silver sponsor in publicity materials and at dinner.)
[] I/We want to be a Bronze Sponsor for $500* with VIP seating for 2.
[] I/We would like to reserve _____ tables(s) of 12 at $1,800 ($900 tax-deductible*)
[] I/We would like to reserve _____ seat(s) at $150 per person ($75 tax-deductible*)
[] I/We are unable to attend. Please accept $_____ as a tax-deductible contribution.

Total: $_____ []Check Enclosed. Please make check to: VCMRF
[]Master Card []Visa

Card Number: _____ Expir. Date: _____
Card Member Name:
Signature:
... October 23, 2001. Please Mail or FAX to (805) 485-0416
Reservations will be held at the door.

CLIENTS. Hannah Roberts, Bryan Wygal
ART DIRECTOR. Hannah Wygal
DESIGNERS. Hannah Wygal, Theresa Veranth
TOOLS. Freehand
PAPER. French Construction
PRINTING. The Press

***Roberts & Wygal wedding invitation

Monster Design

CLIENTS. Carrie Taylor, Kevin McPeek
ART DIRECTORS/DESIGNERS. Lesley Hathaway, Eve Billig
TOOLS. QuarkXPress, Illustrator
PAPER. Synergy Orange Felt (cover), Nekoosa Natural Felt (inside)
PRINTING. Full Circle Press

★★★ "The Daffodil" wedding invitation

A Day in May Design

CLIENTS. Alyson Weenig, Richard Welch
ART DIRECTORS/DESIGNERS. Lesley Hathaway, Eve Billig

TOOLS. QuarkXPress, Illustrator
PAPER. Nekoosa Natural Felt
PRINTING. Full Circle Press

★★★"The Lily" wedding invitation

A Day in May Design

17 JOAN STREET
KENDALL PARK, NEW JERSEY 08824

August
2001

		1	2	3	4	5
6	7	8	9	10	11	10
13	14	15	16	17	18	19
20	21	22	23	24	25	26
27	28	29	30	31		

ANNE MAYER AND SEAN GREGORY
save the date

AgS

AgS

MR. AND MRS. DENIS MAYER
MR. AND MRS. CHRISTOPHER GREGORY
REQUEST THE PLEASURE OF YOUR COMPANY
AT THE MARRIAGE OF THEIR CHILDREN

ANNE ELIZABETH MAYER
AND
SEAN MICHAEL GREGORY

ON SATURDAY THE ELEVENTH OF AUGUST
TWO THOUSAND AND ONE
AT FOUR O'CLOCK
PRINCETON UNIVERSITY CHAPEL
PRINCETON, NEW JERSEY

FOLLOWING THE CEREMONY
PLEASE JOIN US AT THE CAP AND GOWN CLUB
FOR AN EVENING OF DINNER AND DANCING

CLIENTS. Anne Mayer, Cristopher Gregory
ART DIRECTORS/DESIGNERS. Lesley Hathaway, Eve Billig
TOOLS. QuarkXPress, Illustrator
PAPER. Carrara White Feltweave
PRINTING. Full Circle Press

AgS

★★★"The Petunia" wedding invitation
A Day in May Design

CLIENTS. Jennifer Jerde, Daniel Castor
ART DIRECTOR/DESIGNER. Jennifer Jerde
PAPER. Gmund, Cardboard, Wax Paper
PRINTING. Dickson's, Inc.

***Jerde & Castor wedding invitation

Elixir Design

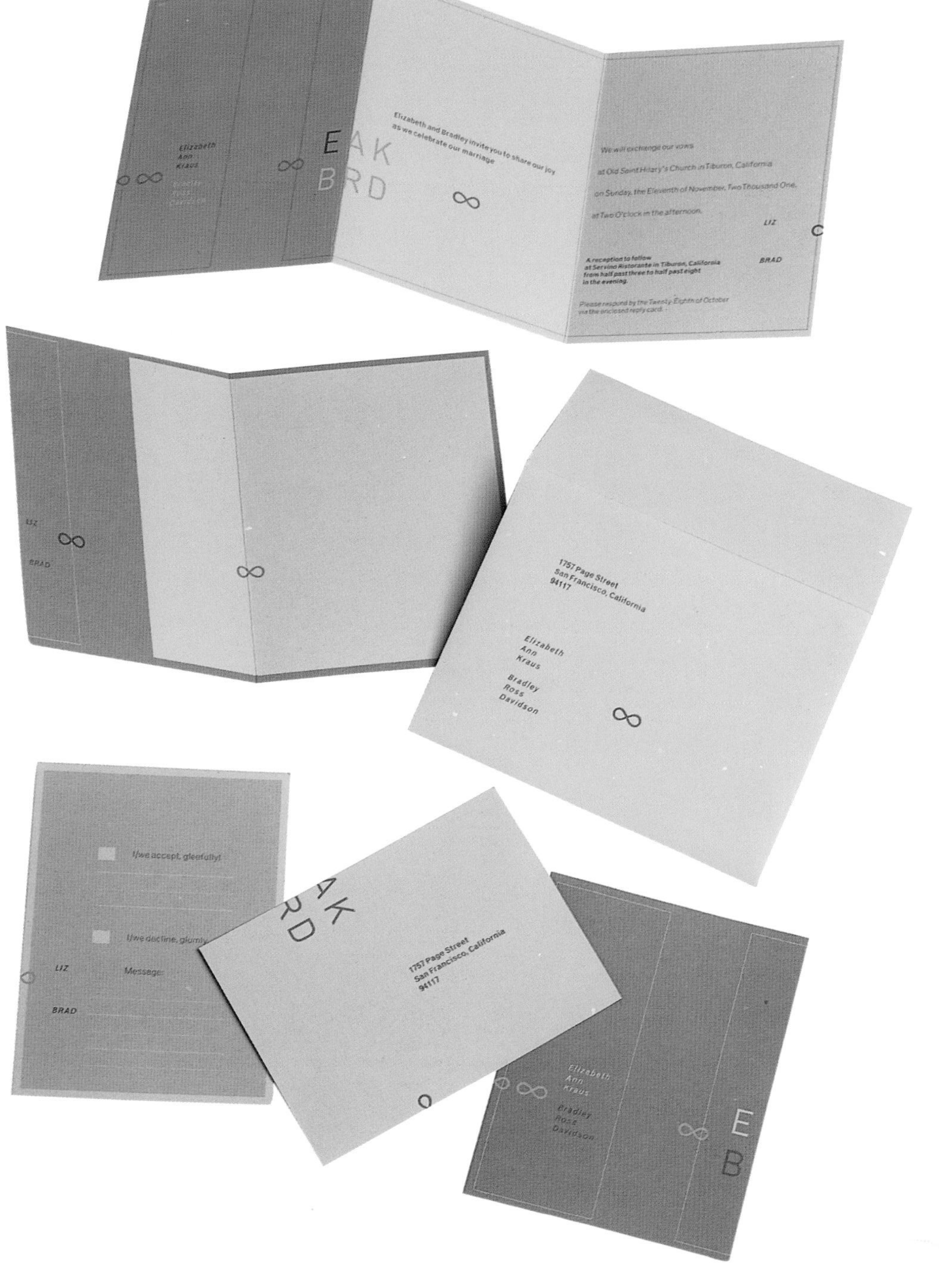

CLIENTS. Brad Davidson, Liz Kraus
ART DIRECTOR. Todd Foreman
DESIGNER. Tessa Lee

TOOLS. Illustrator, Macintosh
PAPER. French Frostone
PRINTING. Quad Express

★★★Davidson & Kraus wedding invitation

Public

CLIENTS. Sharon Allpress, James McQuarrie
ART DIRECTORS/DESIGNERS.
Lesley Hathaway, Eve Billig

TOOLS. QuarkXPress, Illustrator
PAPER. French Construction
PRINTING. Full Circle Press

★★★"The Dahlia" wedding invitation

A Day in May Design

★★★"A Splendid Evening" invitation

ALR Design

CLIENT. Target Margin Theater
ART DIRECTOR/DESIGNER. Noah Scalin
TOOLS. QuarkXPress, Macintosh
PRINTING. Offset

CLIENT. Nassar Design
ART DIRECTOR/DESIGNER. Nelida Nassar

TOOLS. QuarkXPress, Illustrator
PAPER. Cromatica
PRINTING. Silkscreen

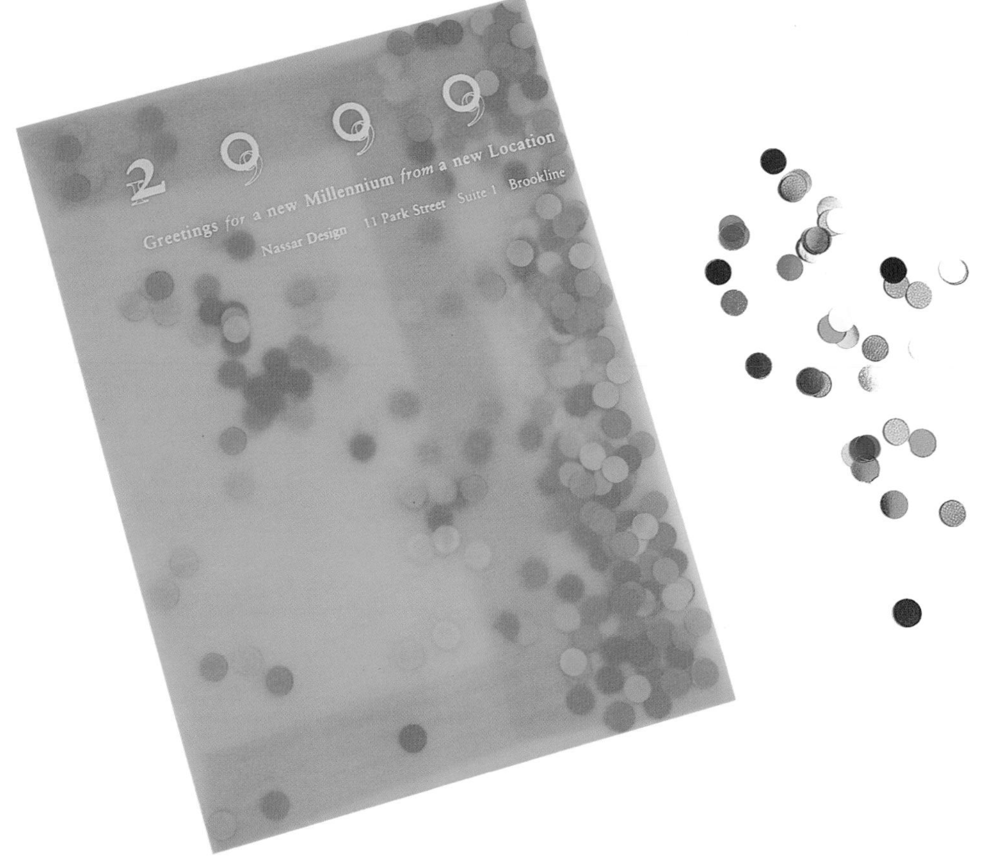

★★★New Millenium greeting

Nassar Design

CLIENT. Red's Restaurant—Chinese Cuisine & Piano Bar
ART DIRECTOR/DESIGNER/ILLUSTRATOR. Warren Welter
TOOLS. QuarkXPress, Illustrator
PRINTING. Technigraphics

1 ★★★Red's One-Year Anniversary invitation

Second Floor

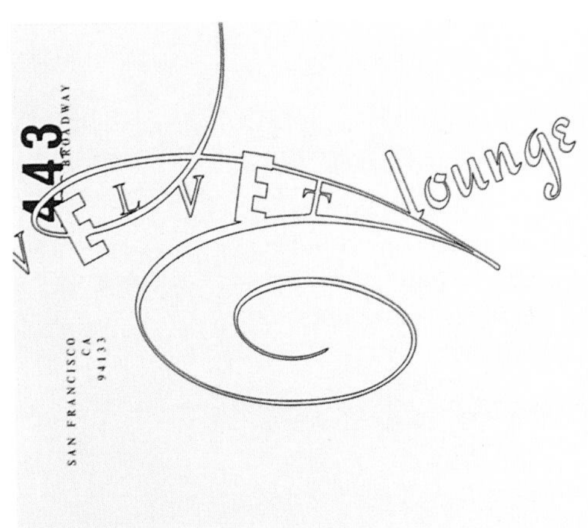

CLIENT. Velvet Lounge
ART DIRECTOR. Steve Barretto
TOOLS. Illustrator, Macintosh

PAPER. Somerset Textured Softwhite 250g/m^2
PRINTING. Classic Letterpress

★★★Velvet Lounge Grand Opening invitation

Flux

tel 415 788 0228

You are cordially invited to attend the

GRAND OPENING of the VELVET LOUNGE

Thursday the fourteenth of May

FEATURING

HOSTED BAR & HOR'DEURVES UNTIL 10PM

INVITATION ONLY | 7 O'CLOCK *to* CLOSING

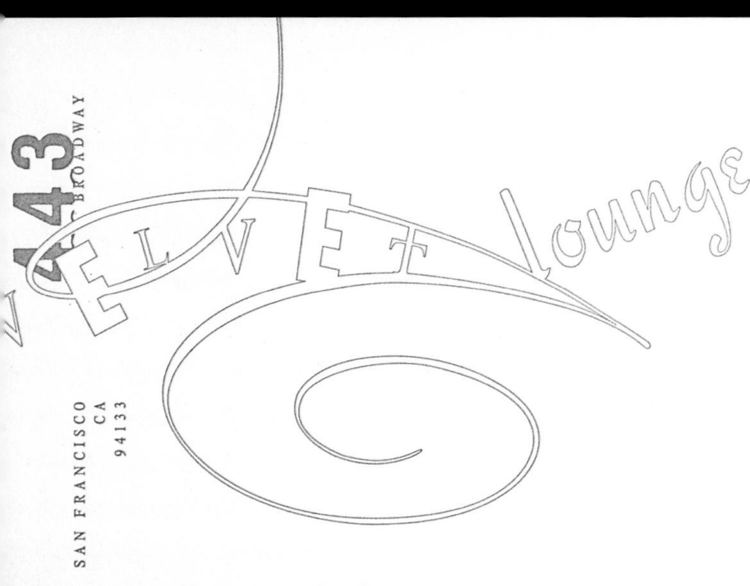

SAN FRANCISCO CA 94133

CLIENT. Kitchen K—A Design Gallery
ART DIRECTORS. Jeff Fabian, Sam Shelton

DESIGNERS. Beth Clawson, Mike Joosse, Jenny Harrington, Scott Rier, Kate Kroener, Natalie Politis, Jackie Ratsch, Beverly Hunter

TOOLS. QuarkXPress, Macintosh
PAPER. Cardboard
PRINTING. Triangle looseleaf

★★★Designed 2 Buy announcement

Kinetik Communication Graphics

CLIENT. Kitchen K—A Design Gallery
ART DIRECTORS. Jeff Fabian, Sam Shelton
DESIGNERS. Beth Clawson, Mike Joosse, Jenny Harrington, Scott Rier, Kate Kroener
TOOLS. QuarkXPress, Macintosh
PAPER. Potlatch McCoy

★★★(50x3) Exhibition announcement

Kinetik Communication Graphics

CLIENT. Fontainebleau Associations
ART DIRECTOR. Michael Graziolo
DESIGNER. Eiji Tsuda

TOOLS. Illustrator, Macintosh
PAPER. Finch Opaque

★★★Fountainebleau poster

Drive Communications

CLIENT. Headlands Center for the Arts
ART DIRECTOR. Jennifer Jerde
DESIGNER. Holly Holmquist
PAPER. 50# White Husky Offset (invite), 80# White Exact Vellum Bristol (reply card), Sundance Felt (A2 and A6 eps)
PRINTING. Norco Printing

★★★Mystery Ball 2000 invitation

Elixir Design

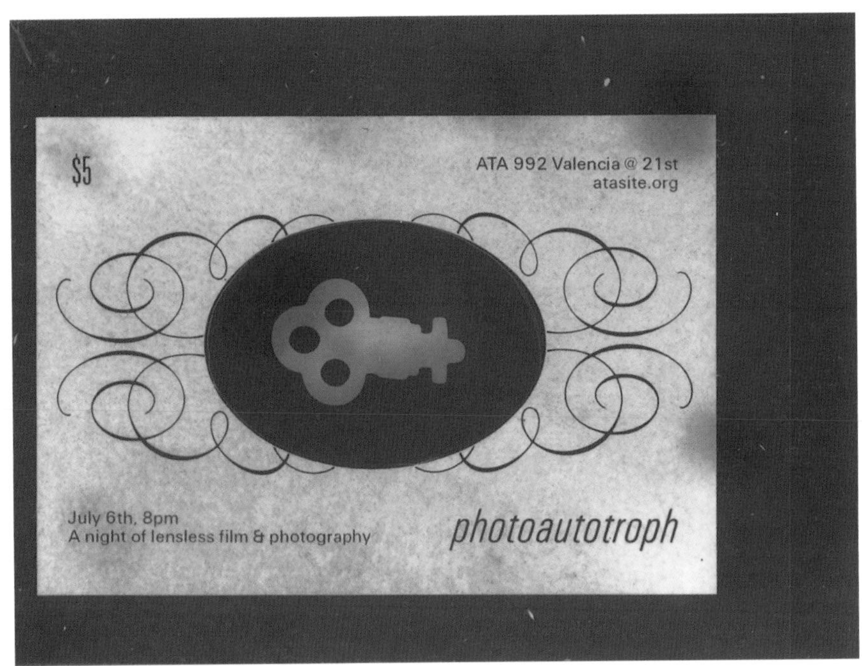

CLIENT. Artists' Television Access (ATA)
ART DIRECTOR. Aaron Cruse
DESIGNERS. Aaron Cruse, Austin Lee, Alexis Bravos

TOOL. Copy camera
MATERIALS. Clip art, small objects, chemistry, sun
PRINTING. Cyanotype (blueprint)

★★★ Photoautotroph invitation

Dead Letter Type

★★★Sagmeister, Inc. Book Presentation invitation

Sagmeister, Inc.

CLIENT. Stefan Sagmeister
ART DIRECTOR/DESIGNER/ ILLUSTRATOR. Stefan Sagmeister
TOOLS. Illustrator, Photoshop
PAPER. Newsprint
PRINTING. Newsprint

CLIENT. Studio Yu
DESIGNER. Jeff Matz

TOOLS. Photoshop, QuarkXPress
PRINTING. Offset, silver ink

★★★Eden invitation

Lure Design, Inc.

PLEASE JOIN US FOR A NIGHT OF DARING TEMPTATIONS ON SATURDAY, OCTOBER 28TH 2000 AT THE SAPPHIRE. PLEASE BE DRESSED TO KILL IN YOUR FAVORITE COSTUME – BE IT FETISH OR FANTASY- AND PRESENT OUR ENCLOSED SIGNATURE FLOGGER FOR ENTRY TO THIS EXCLUSIVE EVENING OF DELIGHT. ENTICING ENTERTAINMENT SHALL BE PROVIDED BY A HOST OF HEAVENLY CREATURES TO SEDUCE YOUR SENSES. SINFUL INFUSIONS WILL BE SERVED TO TANTALIZE YOUR PALATE AND REMOVE YOUR INHIBITIONS. FANTASIES BEGIN REALIZATION AT 11:15PM. $25 IS REQUESTED PER GUEST TO ATTEND THIS EXTREMELY PRIVATE EVENT WITH LIMITED SPACE AVAILABLE. PLEASE CALL 407 592 6949 BY OCTOBER 21ST TO CONFIRM YOUR EXPERIENCE IN THE GARDEN OF EDEN AND TO RECEIVE FURTHER INSTRUCTIONS FOR ENTRY.

Eden

FROM THE EXOTIC TO THE EROTIC

Fairvilla Megastore

5

VOLUME

THE THIRD DIMENSION

packaging / promotions / books / CDs / menus / doorstop

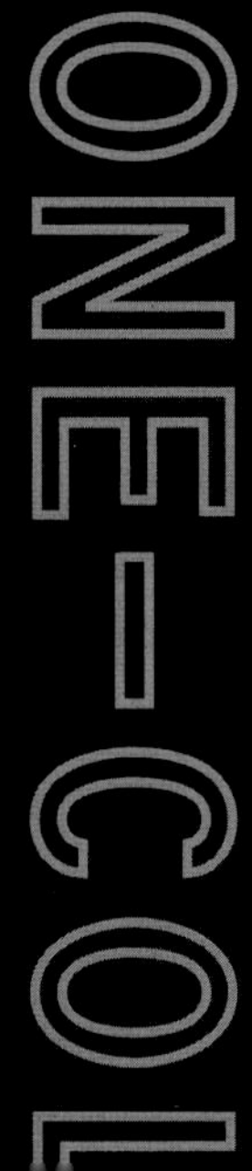

★★★"Sorry We're Open" doorstop

MATTER

CLIENT. MATTER
ART DIRECTORS. Rick Griffith, Jason C. Otero
DESIGNER. Rick Griffith
TOOLS. Illustrator, Macintosh
MATERIALS. Poured plastic, resin, sand
FABRICATOR. James Stoltzenbach

CLIENT. Harvard University Design School
ART DIRECTOR/DESIGNER. Nelida Nassar
TOOL. QuarkXPress
PAPER. Lenticular Film Mounted in Card Stock
PRINTING. Silkscreen

***Hong Kong Defining the Edge
Nassar Design

★★★Pylon party invite

Pylon Design, Inc.

CLIENT. Pylon Design, Inc.
ART DIRECTORS. Scott Christie, Kevin Hoch
DESIGNER. Erin Boyce

TOOLS. QuarkXPress, Macintosh
MATERIALS. Black ink, rubber stamp
PRINTING. Rite Rubber Stamp Company

CLIENT. Pylon Design, Inc.
ART DIRECTORS. Scott Christie, Kevin Hoch
DESIGNER. Scott Christie

TOOLS. QuarkXPress, Macintosh
PAPER. Avery Label
PRINTING. Laser printer

★★★Christmas promo

Pylon Design, Inc.

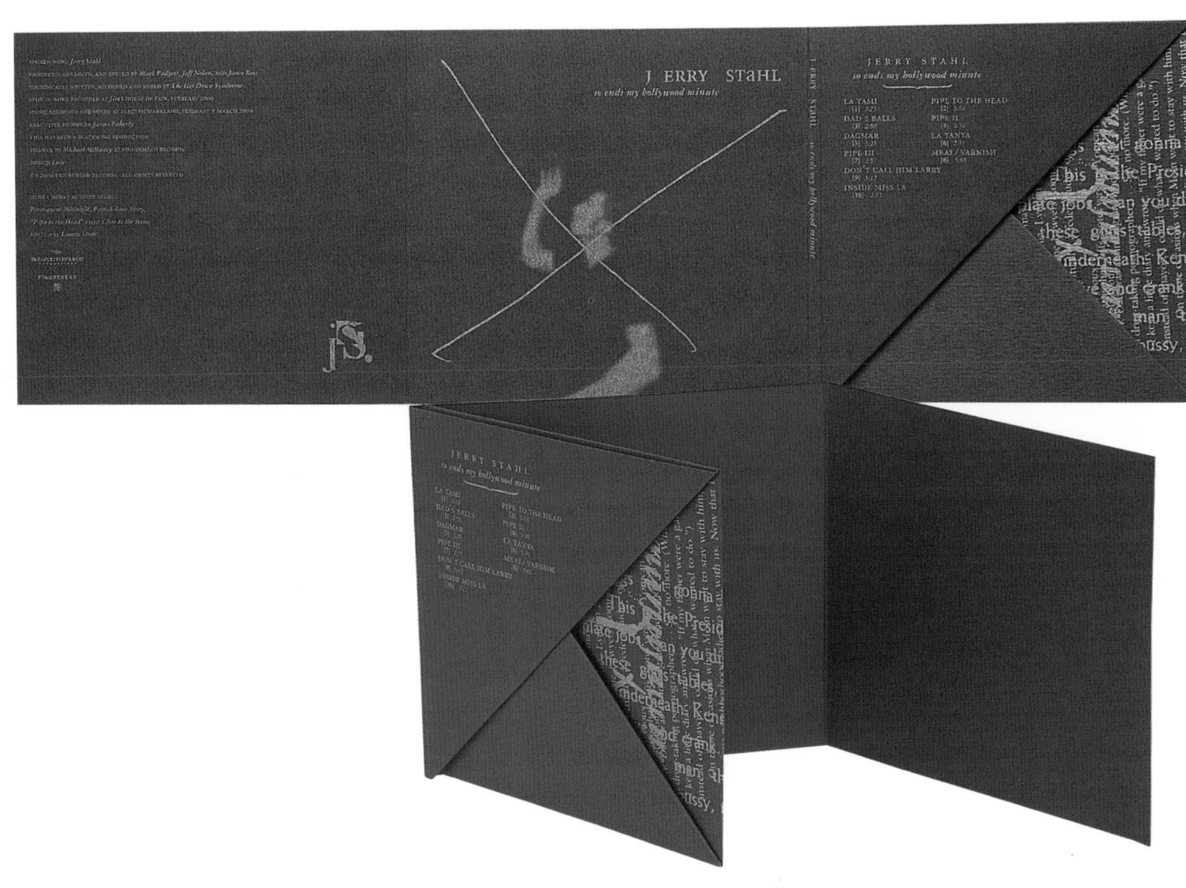

★★★Jerry Stahl CD jacket

Lure Design, Inc.

CLIENT. Figurehead Records
DESIGNER. Jeff Matz
TOOLS. Illustrator, Photoshop

PAPER. Fox River Teton
PRINTING. Offset, silver ink, special fold

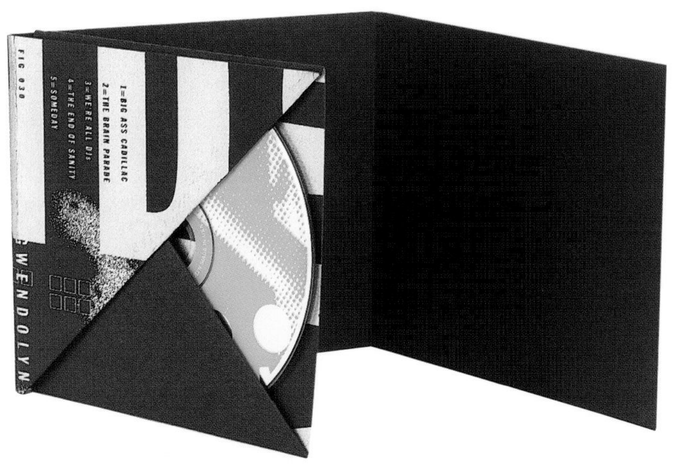

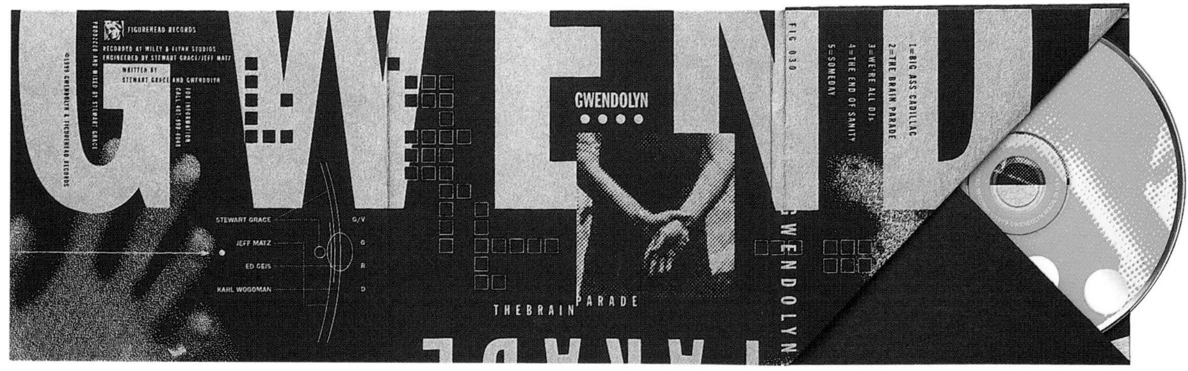

CLIENT. Figurehead Records
DESIGNER. Jeff Matz
TOOLS. Illustrator, Photoshop

PAPER. French Speckletone
PRINTING. Silkscreen, silver ink, special fold

★★★Gwendolyn CD jacket

Lure Design, Inc.

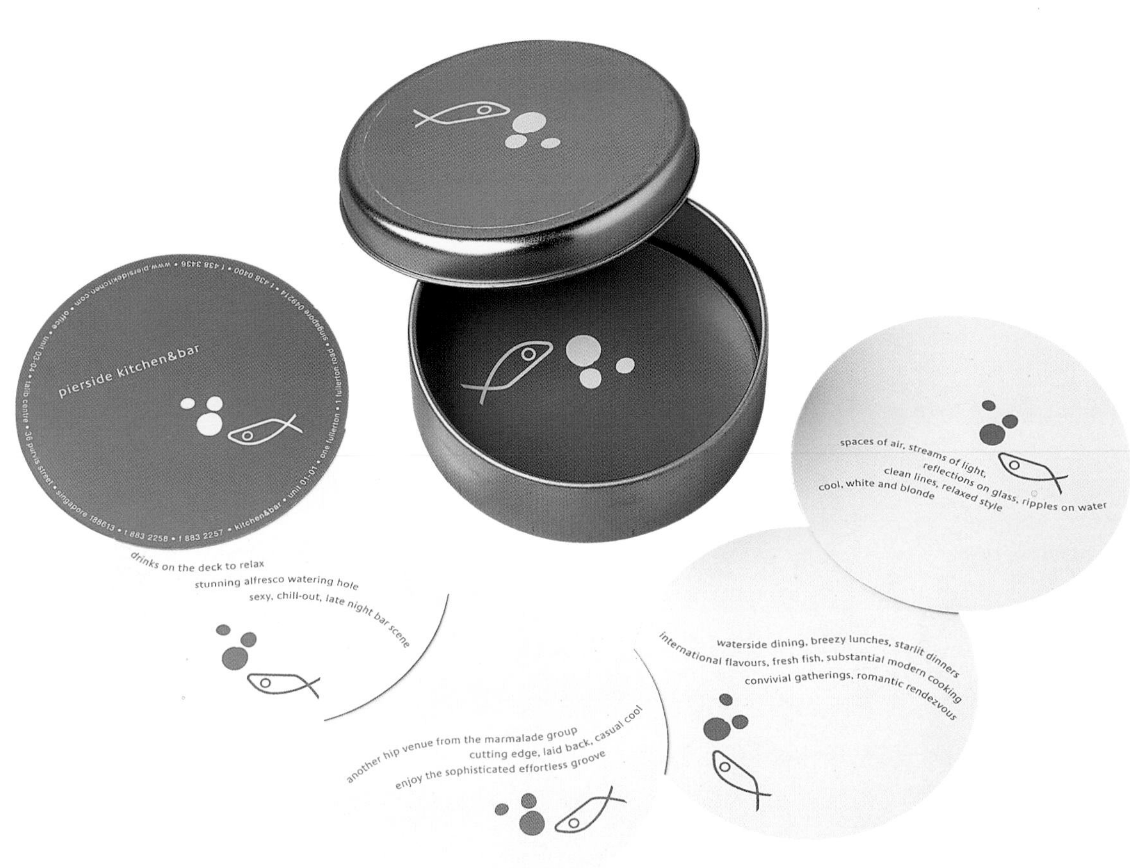

***Pierside media kit

Design Asylum Pte. Ltd.

CLIENT. Pierside Kitchen & Bar
ART DIRECTOR. Christopher Lee
DESIGNER/ILLUSTRATOR. Kai

TOOLS. Freehand, Macintosh
PAPER. Mirrorkote Sticker, Art Card
PRINTING. Metallic Ink

CLIENT. Rossi Ristorante/Enoteca
ART DIRECTOR. Christopher Lee
DESIGNER. Larry Peh
TOOLS. Freehand, Macintosh
PAPER. GSK Transparent/Maple Ivory
PRINTING. Metallic ink

***Rossi Ristorante opening

Design Asylum Pte. Ltd.

VOLUME

162

★★★Caban packaging

Bløk Design

CLIENT. Caban
ART DIRECTOR. Vanessa Eckstein

DESIGNERS. Vanessa Eckstein, Frances Chen, Stephanie Yung

TOOLS. Illustrator, Macintosh
PAPER. Hammermill Via
PRINTING. C.J. Graphics

SENTIAL PILLOWCASES

SET OF TWO / MADE IN INDIA

0 % COTTON POPLIN

WASH DARK COLOURS SEPARATELY.

CHINE WASH COLD

MBLE DRY MEDIUM

BLEACH / NO IRON

caban

caban

caban

L'EAU FROIDE. NE PAS REPAS

SÉCHER PAR CULBUTAGE À MOYENNE TEMPÉRATURE

LAVER À LA MACHINE

NE PAS UTILISER D'AGENT DE BLANCHIMENT.

100% POPELINE DE COT

LAVER LES COULEURS FONCÉES SÉPARÉMENT.

ENSEMBLE DE DEU

FABRIQUÉ EN INDE

CH

100% BR

WASH

MACHIN

HOUSSE

LAVER À LA MACHINE À L

100% CO

SÉCHER PAR CULB

FABRIC

C

★★★Observatory Mansions

Pylon Design, Inc.

CLIENT. Random House of Canada
ART DIRECTOR. Scott Christie
DESIGNERS. Scott Christie, Gary Clement
TOOLS. Pencil, QuarkXPress, Macintosh
PAPER. Matte Coated

superdrug

?regnancy test

1 test • 99% Accurate • Result in 4 minutes

CLIENT. Superdrug
ART DIRECTOR. Garrick Hamm
DESIGNER. Clare Poupard
PRINTING. Lithography

***Pregnancy test packaging

Williams Murray Hamm

CLIENT. Superdrug
ART DIRECTORS. David Turner, Bruce Duckworth
DESIGNER. Janice Davison
TOOLS. Freehand, Macintosh

***Kolor packaging
Turner Duckworth

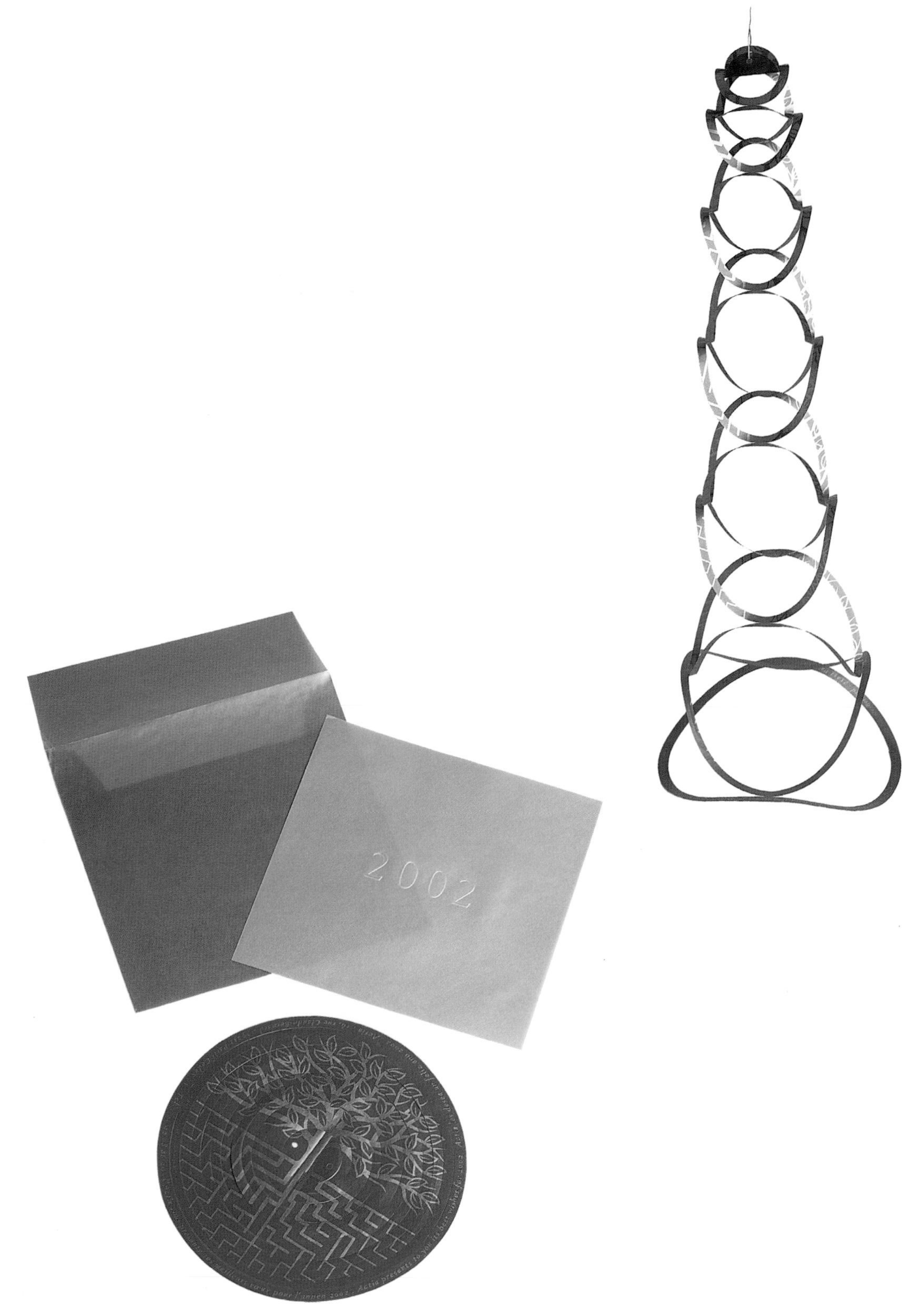

★★★Actia invite

Actia

CLIENT. Actia
ART DIRECTOR/DESIGNER. Anne-Lise Dermenghem
TOOLS. Illustrator, QuarkXPress

PAPER. Thibièrge Évanescent, Comar
PRINTING. Aquaform

CLIENT. Gilbert Paper
ART DIRECTOR/DESIGNER/ ILLUSTRATOR. John Sayles
TOOLS. Illustrator, Macintosh
PAPER. Gilbert Oxford
PRINTING. Offset

★★★"One by One" paper promo

Sayles Graphic Design

★★★Alyson's Valentine promo

Elixir Design

CLIENT. Dickson's, Inc.
ART DIRECTOR. Jennifer Jerde
DESIGNER. Nathan Durrant

PAPER. Crane's Kid Finish Pearl White 134#
PRINTING. Engraved bisque

CLIENT. Locanda Vini & Olii
ART DIRECTOR. Matteo Bologna
DESIGNERS. Andrea Brown, Matteo Bologna
TOOLS. Freehand, Macintosh
PRINTING. Sioux Printing

***Locanda Vini & Olii
Mucca Design

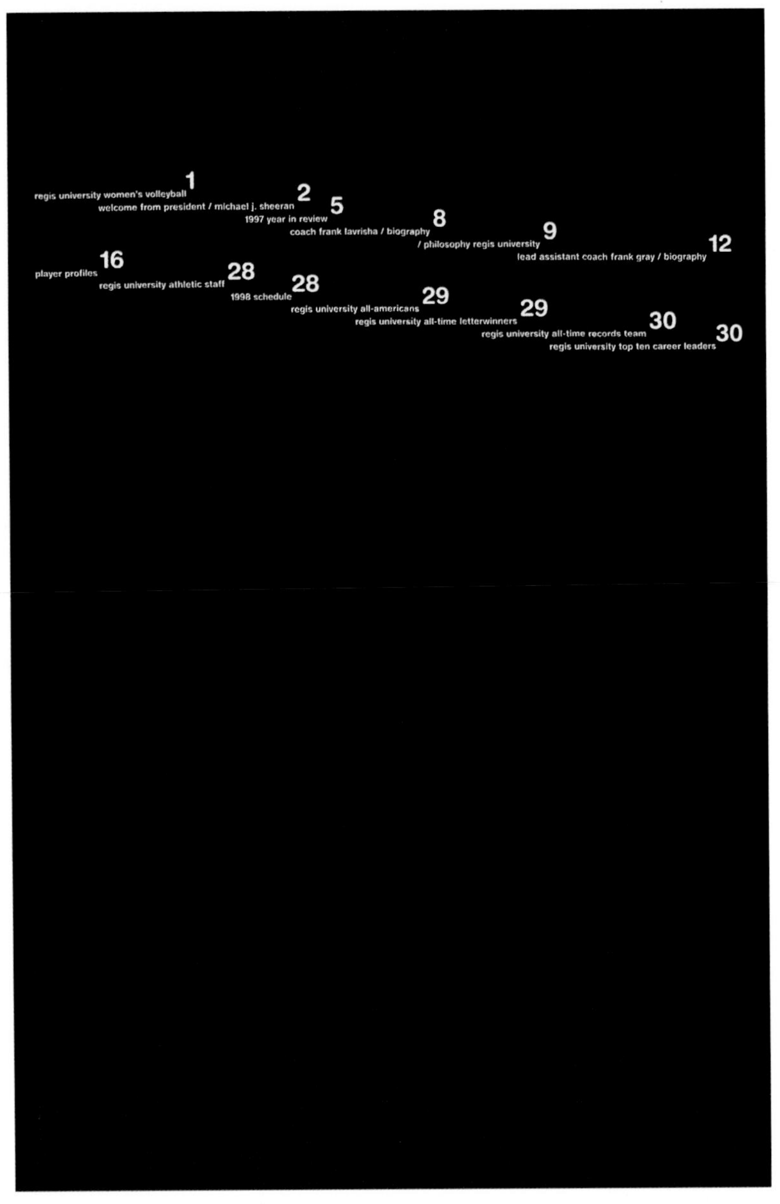

★★★Volleyball book

Jennifer Sterling Design

CLIENT. Regis
ART DIRECTOR/DESIGNER. Jennifer Sterling
PHOTOGRAPHER. Marko Lavrisha

TOOLS. Illustrator, Photoshop
PAPER. Fox River
PRINTING. H. MacDonald Printing

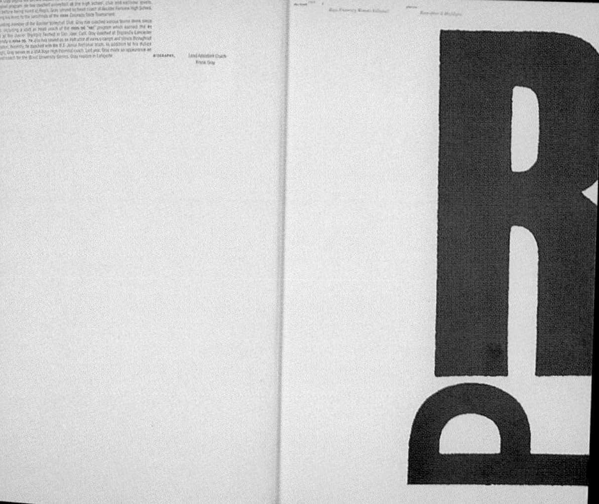

★★★Inkuhnabula Bon-bon box

Liska & Associates

CLIENT. Alyson Kuhn
ART DIRECTOR. Steve Liska
DESIGNER. Christina Nimry

PAPER. Light Impressions Slide Box
PRINTING. Letterpress

CLIENT. Jim Neal Wines
ART DIRECTOR. Tony Auston
DESIGNERS. Tony Auston, Chaim Blomquist, Don Whelan
ILLUSTRATOR. David Laverty
TOOLS. Illustrator, Macintosh
PAPER. Mohawk Superfine Softwhite
PRINTING. Dickson's, Inc.

***Chariot Wine label

Auston Design Group

★★★Instant Best Wishes

@radical.media

CLIENT. @radical.media
ART DIRECTOR/DESIGNER. Rafael Esquer
COPYWRITERS. Angela Fung, Geoff Reinhard
MATERIALS. Canvas Drawstring Bag
TOOLS. Illustrator, Macintosh
PRINTING. Silkscreen, Porcupine Products

CLIENT. @radical.media
ART DIRECTOR/DESIGNER. Rafael Esquer
COPYWRITER. Jon Kamen
MATERIALS. Canvas
TOOLS. Illustrator, Macintosh
PRINTING. Silkscreen, Porcupine Products

★★★Ologi packaging

Turner Duckworth

CLIENT. Golden State International
ART DIRECTORS. David Turner, Bruce Duckworth
DESIGNER. David Turner
TOOLS. Freehand, Macintosh
MATERIALS. Aluminum, Rubber

CLIENT. Heals
ART DIRECTOR. Garrick Hamm
DESIGNER/ILLUSTRATOR. Fiona Curran
PRINTING. Lithography

***Balsamic Vinegar

Williams Murray Hamm

RAPHICS

CDA COLLECTION

ONE-COLOR WORK FROM CHEN DESIGN ASSOCIATES

ONE-COL

182

★★★Kate Madden Yee identity

CLIENT. Kate Madden Yee
ART DIRECTOR. Josh Chen
DESIGNER. Kathryn Hoffman

TOOLS. QuarkXPress, Macintosh
PAPER. Champion Benefit
PRINTING. Full Circle Press

CLIENTS. Jacqueline Quintanilla, Albert Lin
DESIGNER. Max Spector
TOOLS. Illustrator, QuarkXPress, Macintosh
MATERIALS. French Frostone, Crane's Kid Finish, Handmade Paper, Twine, Bead
PRINTING. Full Circle Press (letterpress), Rubber hand stamp (red)

***Quintanilla & Lin wedding invitation

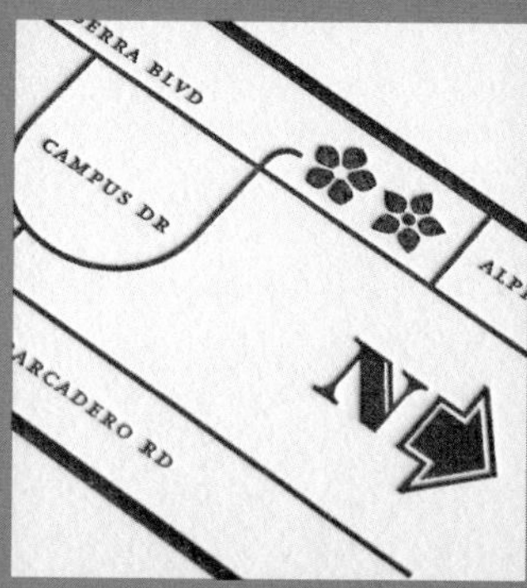

184 ***CED News alumni magazine

CLIENT. College of Environmental Design, UC Berkeley
ART DIRECTORS. Kathryn Hoffman, Josh Chen
DESIGNERS. Max Spector, Kathryn Hoffman

TOOLS. Illustrator, Photoshop, QuarkXPress, Macintosh
PAPER. 60# Hammermill Accent Opaque Lustre White
PRINTING. UC Printing Services

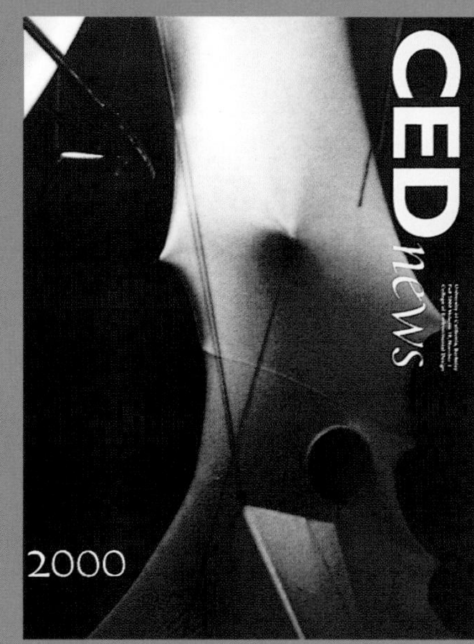

IASTE 2000 THE END OF TRADITION?
BY DAVID MOFFAT, M.ARCH. '90
LESSONS FOR LIFE1
LEARNING FROM STUDENT TRAVEL
BY
Annmarie Adams, M.Arch. '86, Ph.D. Arch. '92
Melissa Harris, M.Arch. '85
Cathy Schwabe, M.Arch. '87

***Maya Spector identity

CLIENT. Maya Spector
DESIGNER. Max Spector
TOOLS. Illustrator, Macintosh
PAPER. Curious Popset, Crane's Crest
PRINTING. Full Circle Press

CLIENT. The Walden School
ART DIRECTOR. Josh Chen
DESIGNERS. Josh Chen, Max Spector, Christopher DeWinter
TOOLS. Illustrator, Photoshop, QuarkXPress, Macintosh
PAPER. Finch
PRINTING. Oscar Printing Company

WITNESS PRODUCTIONS
LOIS MELKONIAN
[415]
350-8161
LM@witnessproductions.org
TELEPHONE
415 383 9703
FACSIMILE
415 388 1916
ADDRESS
96 VIA LOS
TIBURON C
94920

RETURN TO:
96 VIA LOS ALTOS TIBURON CA 94920
WITNESS PRODUCTIONS

CLIENT. Witness Productions, LLC
ART DIRECTOR. Josh Chen
DESIGNER. Max Spector
TOOLS. Illustrator, Macintosh

PAPER. Strathmore Pure Cotton
PRINTING. Oscar Printing Company (offset), Rubber hand stamp (red)

★★★Witness Productions identity

★@RADICAL.MEDIA
435 Hudson Street, 6F
New York, NY 10014 USA
212.462.1500
212.462.1600 f
radicalmedia.com
{176, 177}

★A DAY IN MAY DESIGN
3053 Fillmore Street, #182
San Francisco, CA 94123 USA
415.614.0005
415.614.0006 f
adayinmay.com
{12, 68-69, 133, 134, 135, 138}

★ACTIA
7 rue Édouard Nortier
Neuilly/Seine 92200
FRANCE
+33 14.738.2905
actia.asso.fr
{168}

★ALR DESIGN
3007 Park Avenue, #1
Richmond, VA 23221 USA
804.359.2697
804.359.2697 f
alrdesign.com
{56, 139}

★AMY KNAPP DESIGN
54 Scenic Avenue
San Anselmo, CA 94960 USA
415.482.0541
415.482.0539 f
{43}

★ANVIL GRAPHIC DESIGN
2611 Broadway
Redwood City, CA 94063 USA
650.261.6090
650.261.6094 f
hitanvil.com
{128}

★ARKZIN D.O.O.
Ilica 176/I
Zagreb, HR-10000 CROATIA
+13 85.1.3777 866
+13 85.1.3777 867 f
arkzin.com
{106}

★AUFULDISH & WARINNER
183 The Alameda
San Anselmo, CA 94960 USA
415.721.7921
415.721.7965 f
aufwar.com
{60-61}

★AUSTON DESIGN GROUP
101 S. Coombs Street, Studio P
Napa, CA 94559 USA
707.226.9010
707.226.9013 f
austondesign.com
{29, 175}

★BARBARA BROWN MARKETING & DESIGN
2873 Pierpont Boulevard
Ventura, CA 93001 USA
805.667.6671
805.667.6674 f
bbmd-inc.com
{130-131}

★BECKER DESIGN
225 E. St. Paul Avenue,
Suite 300
Milwaukee, WI 53154 USA
414.224.4942
414.224.4943 f
beckerdesign.net
{42}

★BLØK DESIGN
822 Richmond Street W., #301
Toronto, ON M6J 1C9 CANADA
416.203.0187
416.203.0075 f
{36, 71, 72-73, 162-163}

★BOWHAUS DESIGN GROUPE
340 N. 12th Street, Suite 314
Philadelphia, PA 19107 USA
215.733.0603
215.733.0661 f
bowhausdesign.com
{37}

★CABRA DISEÑO
417 14th Street
San Francisco, CA 94103 USA
415.626.6336
415.626.6330 f
cabradiseno.com
{101-103}

★CAHAN & ASSOCIATES
171 Second Street, Fifth Floor
San Francisco, CA 94105 USA
415.621.0915
415.621.7642 f
cahanassociates.com
{26-27, 58-59}

★CHEEVERS
319 SW Washington, Suite 1200
Portland, OR 97204 USA
503.228.5522
503.228.5521 f
cheevers.com
{116-117}

★CHEN DESIGN ASSOCIATES
589 Howard Street, Fourth Floor
San Francisco, CA 94105 USA
415.896.5338
415.896.5339 f
chendesign.com
{182-183, 184-185, 186, 187, 188-189, 192}

★CHOPLOGIC
2014 Cherokee Parkway
Louisville, KY 40204 USA
502.451.0383
{24}

★DEAD LETTER TYPE
1072 Folsom Street, #452
San Francisco, CA 94103 USA
415.621.4508
deadlettertype.com
{35, 148}

★DECKER DESIGN
14 W. 23rd Street, Third Floor
New York, NY 10010 USA
212.633.8588
212.633.8599 f
deckerdesign.com
{34}

★DESIGN ASYLUM PTE. LTD.
46B Club Street S
(069 423) SINGAPORE
+65 324.8264
+65 324.8265 f
{160, 161}

★DRIVE COMMUNICATIONS
133 W. 19th Street, Fifth Floor
New York, NY 10011 USA
212.989.5103
212.989.6307 f
drivecom.com
{38, 146}

★ELIXIR DESIGN, INC.
2134 Van Ness Avenue
San Francisco, CA 94109 USA
415.834.0300
415.834.0101 f
elixirdesign.com
{16-17, 25, 28, 40, 136, 147, 170}

★ELLEN BRUNI-GILLIES DESIGN
16 Elm Avenue
Kentfield, CA 94904 USA
415.482.8786
415.785.3987 f
{126}

★FLUX
601 Fourth Street, Suite 117
San Francisco, CA 94107 USA
415.974.5034
415.974.0548 f
fluxstudio.com
{22, 46, 47, 142-143}

★FORM FÜNF
Graf Moltke Straße 7
28203 Bremen GERMANY
+49 421 70 30 74
+49 421 70 06 17 f
form5.de
{31-33}

★FRIEDHELM PLASSMEIER
Danziger Strasse 6
Brakel, Westfalia 33034
GERMANY
+49 5.272.8275
+49 5.272.8275 f
{92}

★GEE + CHUNG DESIGN
38 Bryant Street, Suite 100
San Francisco, CA 94105 USA
415.543.1192
415.543.6088 f
geechungdesign.com
{20}

★GEORGE TSCHERNY, INC.
238 East 72nd Street
New York, NY 10021 USA
212.734.3277
212.734.3278 f
{14-15}

★GILLESPIE DESIGN, INC.
32 W. 31st Street, Studio 7
New York, NY 10001 USA
212.239.1520
212.239.1503 f
gillespiedesign.com
{74}

★HOMESPUN DESIGN
1010 D Street
Petaluma, CA 94952 USA
707.766.8058
707.769.8362 f
{127}

★IGOR MASNJAK DESIGN
L'industrie 3
Lausanne, Vaud 1005
SWITZERLAND
41 79.681.7354
{62-67}

★Jeanne Macijowsky Designs
5426 Hermit Terrace
Philadelphia, PA 19128 USA
215.509.7364
215.509.7364 f
{30}

★Jennifer Sterling Design
P.O. Box 475428
San Francisco, CA 94147 USA
415.924.8238
415.924.8448 f
jsterlingdesign.com
{112, 113, 172-173}

★José J. Dias da S. Junior
Rua Nilza M. Martins, 340/103
São Paulo, SP 05628-010
BRAZIL
+55 11.9603.5022
+55 11.3936.4857 f
{23}

★Kinetik Communication Graphics
1436 U Street, NW, Suite 404
Washington, DC 20009 USA
202.797.0605
202.387.2848 f
kinetikcom.com
{144, 145}

★KO Création
6300 avenue du Parc, #420
Montréal, QC H2V 4H8
CANADA
514.278.9550
514.278.7153 f
kocreation.com
{48-49, 50-51, 75}

★Krog
Krakovski Nasip 22
1000 Ljubljana SLOVENIA
+38 6.1.426.5761
+38 6.1.426.5761 f
{129}

★Liska & Associates
515 N. State Street, 23rd Floor
Chicago, IL 60610 USA
312.644.4400
312.644.9650 f
liska.com
{174}

★Love Communications
533 South 700 East
Salt Lake City, UT 84102 USA
801.519.8880
801.519.8884 f
{52-55}

★Lure Design, Inc.
P.O. Box 53144
Orlando, FL 32853 USA
407.835.1699
407.835.1698 f
luredesigninc.com
{19, 96, 97, 98-100, 104, 105, 150-151, 158, 159}

★Matter
1614 15th Street, Fourth Floor
Denver, CO 80202 USA
303.893.0330
303.893.0329 f
matter.ws
{118, 119, 120, 121, 154}

★Mix Pictures Grafik
Weihermatte 5
Sempach CH-6204
SWITZERLAND
+41 41.460.15.45
+41 41.460.15.04 f
mixpictures.ch
{122, 123}

★Mo'Nia
Rua José Rocha 985 R/CH,
Mafamude
Vila Nova De Gaia 4430-122
PORTUGAL
+351 22.379.2295
{76-77}

★Monster Design
P.O. Box 938
Kirkland, WA 98083 USA
425.828.7853
425.576.8055 f
monsterinvasion.com
{132}

★Morla Design
463 Bryant Street
San Francisco, CA 94107 USA
415.543.6548
415.543.7214 f4 f
morladesign.com
{88-91}

★Mucca Design
315 Church Street, Fourth Floor
New York, NY 10013 USA
212.965.9821
212.207.7904 f
muccadesign.com
{57, 171}

★Nassar Design
11 Park Street
Brookline, MA 02446 USA
617.264.2862
617.264.2861 f
{18, 21, 84, 140, 155}

★Niklaus Troxler Design
Postfach
Willisau, CH:6130
SWITZERLAND
+41 41.970.27.31
+41 41.970.32.31 f
troxlerart.ch
{108, 109, 110}

★Public
10 Arkansas, Suite L
San Francisco, CA 94107 USA
415.863.2541
415.863.8954 f
publicdesign.com
{70, 137}

★Pylon Design, Inc.
445 Adelaide Street W.
Toronto, ON M5V 1T1
CANADA
416.504.4331
416.504.4113 f
pylondesign.ca
{39, 156, 157, 164}

★Red Alert Visuals
2455 Folsom Street
San Francisco, CA 94110 USA
415.640.7625
redalertvisuals.com
{114, 115}

★Sagmeister Inc.
222 W. 14th Street, #15A
New York, NY 10011 USA
212.647.1789
212.647.1788 f
stealingeyeballs.net/sagmeister/
{78-81, 82-83, 149}

★Savini Design
106 Walnut Street
San Francisco, CA 94118 USA
415.441.5535
{13}

★Sayles Graphic Design
3701 Beaver Avenue
Des Moines, IA 50310 USA
515.279.2922
515.279.0212 f
saylesdesign.com
{169}

★Second Floor
443 Folsom Street
San Francisco, CA 94105 USA
415.495.3491
415.777.0764 f
secondfloor.com
{141}

★Shoehorn Design
1010 E. 11th Street
Austin, TX 78702 USA
512.478.4190
512.477.5104 f
shoehorndesign.com
{111}

★Studio 455
455 Mariposa Street
San Francisco, CA 94107 USA
415.626.0522
415.626.8922 f
{41}

★Studio International
Buconjićeva 43
Zagreb HR-10000 CROATIA
+385 137.60171
studio-international.com
{94-95}

★Tom & John: A Design Collaborative
1298 Haight Street, #5
San Francisco, CA 94117 USA
415.621.0444
415.551.1220 f
tom-john.com
{85, 93}

★Turner Duckworth
164 Townsend Street, #8
San Francisco, CA 94107 USA
415.495.8691
415.495.8692 f
turnerduckworth.com
{166-167, 178}

★University of Washington School of Art
Visual Communication
Design Program
Box 353440
Art Bldg., Room 102
Seattle, WA 98195-3440 USA
206.685.2773
206.685.1657 f
{107}

★Williams Murray Hamm
Heals Building
Alfred Mews
London W1P 9LB ENGLAND
+44 207.255.3232
creatingdifference.com
{165, 179}

ABOUT THE AUTHOR

Chen Design Associates, San Francisco, was established in 1991 by principal and creative director Joshua Chen. From a one-man basement bedroom operation, CDA has grown into a multi-disiciplinary group that provides strategic vision and creative content for clients in arts and entertainment, education, health care, non-profit, publishing, and technology sectors.

The firm creates work that is conceptually driven, solidly written, passionately designed, and uniquely photographed and illustrated. CDA's body of work includes branding and identity, annual reports, packaging, print collateral, and Web sites.

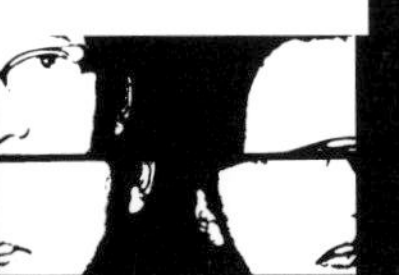

THE STUDIO AT CDA IS A PLACE FOR COLLABORATION, EDUCATION, AND INVENTION. LONGEVITY IS A KEY VALUE THAT EXTENDS TO CDA'S RELATIONSHIP WITH CLIENTS AND VENDORS ALIKE. PRACTICING A PHILOSOPHY OF RESPONSIVENESS AND RELEVANCY, CDA FOSTERS A CREATIVE PROCESS THAT ENGENDERS MUTUAL RESPECT AND UNDERSTANDING WHILE EXCEEDING BUSINESS OBJECTIVES AND PUSHING CREATIVE STANDARDS.

CDA is regularly recognized with national and regional awards for design excellence, including nods from *Print*'s Regional Design Annual, *HOW*'s Self-Promotion and International Design Competitions, The Summit Creative Awards, The Communicator Awards, and the San Francisco Advertising Club. Their work has been selected for inclusion in prominent design books, including *Small Graphics, Touch Graphics: The Power of Tactile Design*, from Rockport Publishers, and the newly published *Graphically Speaking* from HOW Design Books. This is the first book they've authored *and* designed for Rockport Publishers.